AUDIO-VISUAL PATHS TO LEARNING

AUDIO-VISUAL PATH'S TO LEARNING

A COMPARISON OF THREE CLASSROOM METHODS
OF USING EDUCATIONAL SOUND FILMS

By

WALTER ARNO WITTICH, Ph.D.
*Director of the Bureau of Visual Instruction
and Assistant Professor of Education
University of Wisconsin*

and

JOHN GUY FOWLKES, Ph.D.
*Professor of Education
and Dean of the Summer Session
University of Wisconsin*

New York   London

HARPER & BROTHERS PUBLISHERS

AUDIO-VISUAL PATHS TO LEARNING

Copyright, 1946, by Harper & Brothers

All rights in this book are reserved. No part of the book may be reproduced in any manner whatsoever without written permission except in the case of brief quotations embodied in critical articles and reviews. For information address Harper & Brothers

H-X

CONTENTS

INTRODUCTION	vii
PREFACE	ix

CHAPTER I

The Development of the Motion Picture	1
The Place of the Silent and Sound Motion-Picture Film in the Classroom	6
Directed or Undirected Seeing	21

CHAPTER II

Description of the Experiment	29
The Statistical Technique	49

CHAPTER III

Experimental Results and Interpretation	55
Gains Made on Specific Educational Sound Films	65
Is There a Relationship Between Aptitude and the Child's Ability to Observe and Learn from Educational Sound Films?	66
Correlation Between Reading Grade and Test Scores	69
Homogeneity of the Groups Increased by the Use of Experimental Factors 2 and 3	72
Summary	72

CHAPTER IV

Pupil Reactions to Sound Films	76

CHAPTER V

Summary of the Entire Investigation	96
LITERATURE CITED	101

APPENDIX A. Learning Guide Used with Experimental Factors 2 and 3 105

APPENDIX B. Summaries of Nine Rotations for Three Grades for the 27 Films, and Tests for the Statistical Significance of the Differences Between the Means of Performance for Experimental Factors 1, 2, and 3 117

INTRODUCTION

Of all the important areas of research in the field of audio-visual instruction, probably the most neglected has been that of film utilization. While this area offers great opportunity for creative research, at the same time it requires the most painstaking and laborious work on the part of the researcher. The "traditional" techniques of evaluation research do not always provide the types of data required to formulate defensible conclusions in this area. The present study has undertaken to discover the relative effectiveness of several methods of integrating the film with classroom activities. The nature of these methods made difficult the control of the time factor. However, this study shows that the manner in which the film is introduced into the classroom and utilized thereafter is a most significant, if not the determining, factor in effective film use. It is to be hoped that, as research techniques in this area are refined, further studies will show that the striking differences in mastering film content outweigh the significance of the time factor. The work of Drs. Wittich and Fowlkes should challenge teachers to make every effort to realize the full potentiality of the classroom film as a superior aid to learning.

V. C. ARNSPIGER, Vice-President,
Encyclopædia Britannica Films, Inc.

PREFACE

During recent years the use of silent and sound films in schools has increased sharply, and it seems highly probable that in the near future text films will be used in thousands rather than in hundreds of schools as is now the case. Studies have been made which establish the place of the film as a tested instrument to supplement good classroom techniques now in use. However, only a small minority of schools have a well-planned, balanced program of film use.

Just beginning to attract the attention of educators is the problem of utilizing this newest supplement to good classroom techniques to the fullest possible extent. Up to the present, little attention has been given this problem—and understandingly so. Because the first films used in the nation's classrooms produced such apparently successful results, little or no thought has been given to the possibility of achieving further gains in the assimilation of information and the development of attitudes through using films more efficiently. Such problems as the relation between directed attention and the viewing of teaching films, the effect of vocabulary study in anticipation of such films, and the role of discussion, self-evaluation, and other summarizing techniques, have received little attention. The present report concerns one attempt to formulate more effective methods of using teaching films in the classroom.

The present investigators advance the premise, based on valid research, that the teaching or text film makes a valuable contribution to learning situations in the classroom. This premise established, their study develops and tests three methods of using such a film to its greatest advantage in the classroom. As such, the present investigation is a pioneer in a new area of research in audio-visual aids. Similar studies of other aids will result in still more effective methods of utilization.

Enthusiasm for the text film should not lead to the neglect of many other important techniques in visual education. Throughout this volume the point is repeatedly made that the selection of the visual aid, or combination of aids, best adapted to the purpose at hand is vital and that films should be used only when certain conditions are satisfied. Other aids, such as maps, charts, slides, posters, models, study guides, blackboards, mockups, variations of the filmstrip, recordings, and in some cases elaborate devices evolved to provide synthetic experience, must be understood and used just as the skilled craftsman selects the correct tool required for a particular operation.

Advances in the audio-visual field have been dramatic. What was once the magic lantern has become that very modern instrument, the opaque projector, attached to whose lens is a camera shutter that compels quick analysis of projected objects. Maps, charts, and diagrams are no longer neglected dust catchers of the schoolroom but have become bold schematic assemblies for the analysis of complex mechanisms. They incorporate exploded views and third-dimensional moving parts. The models formerly available only in awkward cardboard are now made from clear and colored plastics in sections that can be easily separated. The filmstrip is no longer just a series of still-picture discards, but a sequence of well-integrated color views and diagrams, with properly spaced multiple-choice questions and answers. A streamlined projector moves the filmstrip from one frame to the next at the flick of a button and includes a microphone and loud-speaker to project the voice of the lecturer-operator. This projector also has a sound arm and automatic turntable on which may be played sixteen-inch recordings synchronized with the filmstrip frames. Efficient optical viewers that only remotely resemble the parlor stereopticon of earlier days provide third-dimensional depth for photographic prints.

The fact that these and many other audio-visual aids have reached an advanced stage has led to their further development by the Army and Navy. Although their original motivation was the necessity for speed in training large numbers of men, the Armed Services were quickly impressed by the higher quality of training that resulted. Audio-visual aids made it possible to send the very best in instructional method anywhere in the world; retention of information was increased, and skills were taught much more quickly and were better understood. This phase of the program was so successful that professionally trained utilization officers were commissioned to implement the efforts of the production and distribution personnel. This utilization group has profited from untold experience in the largest laboratory ever available in the history of visual education. Within the limits of matériel restrictions, but in answer to the similar demands of war production training and teacher shortages, this advancement has been paralleled in schools and universities.

These broader aspects of the field of audio-visual aids although not the immediate concern of this study, are, however, related to the methods herein presented as the best means of adapting text films to the learning process. It is hoped that these methods will prove helpful to all who use teaching films.

Madison, Wisconsin WALTER A. WITTICH
November, 1945 JOHN GUY FOWLKES

AUDIO-VISUAL
PATHS
TO LEARNING

CHAPTER I

THE DEVELOPMENT OF THE MOTION PICTURE

In 1894 at an exhibition open to the New York public, Thomas Edison exhibited a strange machine called the Kinetoscope, in competition with another instrument, the magic lantern. Most of the attention was concentrated on the magic lantern, which projected a fixed image upon a screen for all the group to see. The Kinetoscope actually gave motion to one image projected upon an internal screen, but the image could be viewed only by the individual. When Edison was asked why he would not devote his efforts to projecting the moving image on a screen so that more than one person could view it at a time, he is alleged to have said, "If I do that, I'd ruin the market for my magic lantern." Typical of his first feelings toward his Kinetoscope was the fact that he omitted to patent his device in countries outside the United States (30).[1]

While Edison is usually credited with the invention of the first workable motion picture and while, as the result of his first public exhibition, hundreds of these machines were sold, his contribution was largely a refinement upon the earlier work of such men as Dr. E. J. Marey and Edward Muybridge, who in 1872 at Palo Alto, California, secured the first sequence of still pictures which in their composite traced at split-second intervals the movements of a race horse as it moved down the track and tripped the thread shutters of 24 cameras placed along the adjacent railing (13).

The man who discovered the medium which made it possible to take pictures with such speed as to record not only the original impression but later to project these images at

---

[1] Bold-face numbers in parentheses refer to items in the bibliography on p. 101.

split-second intervals was the Reverend Hannibal Goodwin, who in 1889 discovered celluloid. This was almost immediately recognized by George Eastman as the medium through which the commercially perfected positive film could be developed.

From that time on, the first crude experimentation in the projection of motion-picture sequences traveled a divided road. In one direction, Dr. Marey accomplished the filming and study of scientific fields which heretofore had been a mystery. Films of the flight of insects, the locomotion of animals in water, the heart in action, and the circulatory system of animals opened up vistas for scientific study whose results answered questions that had caused doubt, uncertainty, and even malpractice. Dr. Marey's experiments in photographing the action of the heart, M. J. Carvallo's success in harnessing X-ray to motion pictures, and Dr. J. Comandon's success in developing microphotography are but a few examples of how this amazing new technique of photography gave impetus to scientific research for the betterment of mankind. Well known are the development of the motion picture and the furtherance of the educational campaign under the direction of the Department of Agriculture and the Department of the Interior. Also well known is the contribution made by motion-picture photography to the success of campaigns planned and undertaken by the Allied forces during World War 1.

In the other direction, the nickelodeon was casting its spell over seventy-five million Americans. Following in the footsteps of Europeans, who were quick to realize the opportunities of the early cinema, American producers first made 50-foot lengths of film which gradually gave way to 1000-foot reels of the Corbett-Fitzsimmons fight in Carson City and the 3000-foot Oberammergau Passion Play exhibited as early as 1897. During the first decade of the twentieth century, such themes as Jules Verne's *Trip to the Moon, The Great Train Robbery, Trapped by Blood Hounds,* or *The Lynching at Cripple Creek* were common to the dreams and ambitions of youth everywhere in the United States. And while breath-taking one-reel melodramas flickered their images to the accompaniment of a reader of an automaton-like pianist in hundreds of movie houses, pioneer "legions of decency" met at adjacent public halls and churches to debate the moral values of the movies and wonder where the trend of the times was leading.

Entertainment films prospered, huge profits were made, research was begun, and the quality of the photography was improved. In entertainment films were developed most of the technological improvements which have since been used advantageously by the producers of scientific and educational films. Giving up his original leadership, the educational and scientific researcher was satisfied with adapting commercial improvements to his own use. The entertainment film producers assumed a leadership which led to the development of the Vitaphone in 1925, and which prompted Theodore Case and Dr. Lee De Forest to adapt the bewildering properties of the photoelectric eye to the problem of synchronizing sound and image. Although 1924 to 1930 can be described as the period of commercial sound adaptation, it was not until the end of this period that the producers of educational films were certain enough of its possibilities to adapt this technique to use in the classroom.[2]

Between 1918 and 1930 many educators bent their energies toward evaluating the possibilities of the motion-picture film in making the educative process more meaningful. They examined the scientific films produced early in the century and challenged the educational value of the entertainment film which trades upon sensationalism, glamour, the eternal

[2] For a further discussion of this period of development, see Franklin (15).

triangle, and escape. Educators looked askance at the early documentary film, which, while basically holding to the development of a story, a process, a social need, or a reform, often does not consider its task completed until it has left its audience in a white heat of enthusiasm and resolved to take action in a direction not always socially desirable. Teachers have questioned the advertising or commercially prepared film which, although allegedly suitable for classroom use, certainly does not fulfill its responsibility to the producer until it has subtly or otherwise put across a sales "plug" or a drive to action, or has consciously sought a change in attitude. Furthermore, teachers have lost faith in the enthusiast of the moment who, seeing some possibilities in the motion-picture film, suddenly becomes such an avid protagonist that he attempts to convert all factual material, all elements of learning, and all experience into this medium.

Research, therefore, has attempted to meet the responsibility of establishing the answers to such questions as: "What will motion pictures do that good, traditional classroom technique will not accomplish?" "What will the addition of sound to the silent motion picture do which neither silent film nor traditional classroom work will accomplish?" "What will motion pictures do above and beyond what class discussions, lectures, lantern slides, filmstrips, and textbooks can accomplish?"

The researcher of the 1918–1924 period had to work with materials which today seem inadequate. Since that time, however, great advances have been made in the quality of motion-picture films and projectors as well as in educational film planning and editing. A review of the outstanding educational research between 1918 and 1930, which was carried on with silent motion pictures, and that between 1930 and 1935, in which classroom experiments with sound motion pictures were introduced, reveals such limitations as these:

1. Several experiments in the classroom use of motion-picture films began with the explanation that the films were the best that could be secured, but that they were not essentially educational films. When cuttings from entertainment films, safety films produced by railroad lines and automotive corporations, travelogues released by steamship lines, or industrial process films produced by manufacturing companies are used, the place of the true educational film in the classroom is not being investigated. The true educational film observes a teaching philosophy, a logical sequence, and the unfolding of ideas and processes, factors which are usually ignored in the good-will films of commercial organizations that attempt to emphasize the identity of the company and its service or product. Films used in some of the early experiments can thus be challenged as to the degree to which they fit the curriculum and the children's interests, and the school children's readiness to absorb the type of information presented.

2. Similar comments can be made concerning experimentation which has involved comparison of sound and silent films. Some experimenters simply added recorded lectures to silent films and called the latter "sound films." It has since been recognized that the true sound film is not the silent film accompanied by a recorded lecture but rather a motion-picture film whose sound track includes environmental sounds—the lowing of cattle, the whir of the turbine, the clanking of heavy machinery, the creaking and swishing of the vanes of Dutch windmills, the crunching of icebergs and the moaning of the wind in the Arctic, the sounds of the countryside and of canal boats in England, or the happy laughter of children who live in Hawaii and South America. In the true educational motion picture, sound is used only when its inclusion will make more vivid the actual social or

living conditions characteristic of the section of life or area of production being portrayed.

3. A third indictment can be leveled against the early sound films which were specifically produced for use in experimental studies. In some instances a well-handled, traditional classroom demonstration or activity was reproduced as a motion picture. Little or no thought was given to the criterion which should underlie the production of any motion picture—the fact that the motion-picture technique should be used for illustrating only those aspects of life which other techniques are less capable or incapable of depicting. The fact that truly educational pictures have been developed only since 1925 limited research prior to that time because of the absence of experimental situations under which such films could be evaluated.

With these few points in mind, an attempt will be made to review research efforts in the field of motion-picture and sound films.

The Place of the Silent and Sound Motion-Picture Film in the Classroom

If a roll of the pioneers in the field of visual education could be drawn up, it would probably begin with the names of David Sumstine, Joseph Weber, F. Dean McCloskey, and Frank Freeman. These men, and others, plunged into the wilderness of untried techniques and tools with the determination to discover, if they could, the character, function, advantages, and possible effective uses of this new and promising adjunct to classroom method. Their initial research was carried on between 1918 and 1924. It was during this period that the first comparisons between visual and traditional methods of classroom presentation were made. This was also the era of Weber's research which inquired, "Are visual aids merely a fad or do they have a distinct value?" and of Freeman's first comprehensive survey, in the form of thirteen separate studies, which investigated the effectiveness of the silent film under varying classroom procedures and in competition with other traditional mediums and opened broader vistas for research and experimentation. Some of the earliest investigators introduced artificial and atypical teaching techniques in their attempt to place the motion picture properly. More often than not, poor films were chosen; many of them were entertainment or advertising films. Experimental investigations which deviated from the normal courses of study were not uncommon. Experimental groups were often too small to reveal significant data, and many generalizations based upon such evidence withstood only briefly the assault of subsequent research.

The second period of research, 1924 to 1930, was marked by the continuing work of Frank Freeman (16), Daniel Knowlton (22), J. Warren Tilton (22), Ben Wood (36), and investigators in England, who succeeded in removing many of the unsatisfactory conditions present in the earlier studies. In addition to substantiating further the function of the motion-picture film in the classroom, these men attempted to determine to what extent the new technique motivated pupil activity, increased the learner's reception of factual information, and promoted or strengthened his ability to understand causes and relationships.

The advent of the sound film after 1930 gave rise to another cycle of experimental research. Beginning with the investigations of Frances Consitt (9), Varney Arnspiger (4), C. C. Clark (8), Phillip Roulon (31), William Westfall (34), Harry Wise (35), John Elmore Hansen (18), and including such recent studies as those of David Goodman (17) and others, much of the research has dealt with the sound film in its relation to informational learning and developmental thinking, to effective use of the silent film, and to effective and tested traditional classroom procedure. Research during this last period has observed the premise that sound and silent films, when used in the classroom, must be valid; i.e., (1) they must present information which is specifically adapted to the technique of motion and sound, and (2) they must present a given field of information better than other mediums such as slides, charts, textbooks, demonstrations, or lectures.

The researches just cited have stood the tests of time, of the application of these techniques to closely allied subject-matter areas, and of the examination and criticism of other research workers. The findings of these researches will be drawn upon in stating and answering the following twelve questions:

1. In what subject-matter areas have investigations been made relative to the effective classroom use of educational sound and silent films?

2. Has the educational silent film been proved a useful adjunct to classroom method?

3. Has the educational sound film been proved a useful adjunct to classroom method?

4. Is information learned through educational sound and silent films retained more or less effectively than when learned through other methods of classroom instruction?

5. Are educational sound and silent films more effective with children of low or of high ability?

6. Do educational sound and silent films stimulate general interest?

7. What effect does the use of educational silent and sound films have upon the voluntary reading done by children?

8. What is the age beyond which educational sound and silent films can be effectively used?

9. What is the contribution of the educational sound and silent film in terms of factual learning and of learning which effects changes in the social living of children?

10. What effect does the educational sound and silent film have upon the oral response of those who view them?

11. How much more effective are educational sound films than educational silent motion pictures in helping students gain new information?

12. Are educational sound and silent films more advantageous when shown to classroom-sized groups or to auditorium-sized groups?

1. In what subject-matter areas have investigations been made relative to the effective classroom use of educational sound and silent films?

No one comprehensive survey has been made. Perhaps Freeman's thirteen studies on the silent film (16), mentioned above, came as close as any. His research was conducted in the social studies, penmanship, physics, home economics, English, and health education; all of it revealed that the essential value of the silent film was its ability to depict processes involving motion. Goodman (17) showed the value of the sound film in the field of safety education. Eichel (11) demonstrated the unusual persistence of a visual image gained through a sound film in the retention of learning relative to current history. Arnspiger (4) conclusively tested and established the advantage of the sound film in the music field. In general science, Krasker (23), Roulon (31), Arnspiger (4), and Wood and Freeman (36) definitely established the advantages of well-selected sound and silent films over traditional classroom techniques. Hansen (19) proved the superiority of certain sound films over non-sound films in tenth-grade biology. Consitt (9), Knowlton and Tilton (22), and Wise (35) indicated the type of film used most advantageously in the field of history, as well as the method of its use. In his experimental research at the college level in the scientific field, Clark (8) demonstrated the effectiveness of the sound film. A large portion of the subject matter in the elementary, junior, and senior high schools and at the college level has been probed. In every case the advantage of true educational sound and silent motion pictures has been demonstrated when they have been properly used under conditions which warrant their use.

2. Has the educational silent film been proved a useful adjunct to classroom method?

The researches of Westfall (34), Roulon (31), Clark (8), Consitt (9), Wood and Freeman (36), Knowlton and Tilton (22), and Weber (33) provided evidence of the positive contribution to learning made by the silent film. Roulon (31) declared that the best short summary which can be made of 100 separate experiments is that the educational motion picture, when properly produced and wisely used, possesses distinct pedagogical values over and above traditional teaching methods upon which the same amounts of time and energy are expended. Clark (8) concluded that, at the college level, sound and silent films in the physical sciences are as effective as lecture demonstrations in developing ability to think and to reason. According to Consitt (9), the historical film gives life to the past by making historical characters come alive, giving background to historical events, recreating atmosphere, and portraying life in motion. Such a film corrects, clarifies, and simplifies previous knowledge. It portrays details not found in textbooks which are often taken for granted by the teacher. These films offer vicarious experience for children who have had no opportunities to travel and have no library or museum facilities.

Wood and Freeman's investigation (36) in the field of geography showed gains of 33 per cent of one standard deviation for the experimental groups that had the advantage of seeing silent motion-picture films. An advantage of 15 per cent of one SD was claimed in general science. Knowlton and Tilton (22) reported that seventh-grade pupils in the experimental groups learned 19 per cent more with the aid of historical motion pictures and retained 12 per cent more than the control groups. They reported also that the general progress of the experimental group was slightly higher than that of the control group. This information is significant because it establishes the fact that progress was not made at the expense of the work regularly covered during the school term.

According to Freeman (16), the motion-picture film offered the most outstanding advantages when the presentation of information demanded motion to illustrate it. Since motion was found to make objects more interesting, the resulting heightened interest fostered closer attention which, in turn, brought about more learning and increased permanence in learning. He pointed out that for many purposes traditional methods of teaching were just as effective as the silent film, and certainly in those instances the use of the silent film depended on the judgment of the teacher. Freeman also found that the value of the motion picture varies inversely to the child's previous acquaintance with the object of study or to his experiences that nearly parallel it. Weber (33) discovered that better results were obtained when lessons were accompanied by films than when traditional teaching techniques were followed. One caution must always be observed, however; i.e., the true silent film is of value only when it can present a process or a social situation more effectively than any other medium of disseminating information to the child in the classroom.

3. Has the educational sound film been proved a useful adjunct to classroom method?

Here, as in the case of the silent film, the educational

sound film has been conclusively proved an asset to classroom method. Such investigators as Wise (35), Eichel (11), Roulon (31), Clark (8), and Arnspiger (4) pointed out the advantage of these films to immediate and retained learning in such subjects as American history, safety education, general science, biological and physical science, natural science, and music, at elementary, high school, and college levels.

Eichel (11) concluded from his findings that the advantage of the sound film lies in the degree to which the audio-visual image persists over long periods of time in the child's mind. He stated that the sound film assists the child by helping him retain concepts and information which he has viewed and heard. Wise (35) found that the results of his studies indicated that the use of the motion picture in teaching history can and does increase the amount of information which the student possesses. His experiments demonstrated that the teaching technique in which the Chronicles of America Photoplays were used was more effective from the instructional standpoint than the usual mode of presentation. In summarizing results of his study at the college level, Clark (8) reported that the educational sound film in which sound is a vital and realistic part of the picture was as effective as identical lecture demonstrations in conveying specific information in the field of physical science and was effective in developing ability to think and to reason.

Arnspiger (4), reporting on the performance of elementary school children in Grades 5 and 7, said that in average gains for all the children taking part in his experiment the experimental groups showed superiorities which ranged from 22 to 30 per cent in natural science units and from 18 to 34 per cent in music units. The averages made on the non-picture items indicated that the marked superiority of the experimental groups was produced without sacrificing the subject matter not specifically presented by the talking picture. He concluded that the talking pictures used in the experiment made marked and lasting contributions to learning in both natural science and music units, and that these contributions were made without loss as far as learning other elements of the units not included in the talking pictures was concerned.

4. Is information learned through educational sound and silent films retained more or less effectively than when learned through other methods of classroom instruction?

Experimental evidence advanced by Eichel (11), Roulon (31), Arnspiger (4), Consitt (9), Hansen (18), Knowlton and Tilton (22), and Weber (33) pointed to positive advantages in the direction not only of learning and using information included in the films but more definitely in retaining this information over long periods of time. Eichel (11) reported that the advantage of the sound film used in connection with the teaching of current events was shown most conclusively ten days, ten weeks, and a year after the film was seen. In his study of the sound film used with tenth-grade students of biology, Hansen (18) could discern a higher level of retention among children in the experimental group who had seen the sound film in its entirety than in two other groups. Roulon (31) stated that, in terms of retention, the results of his experiment indicated great superiority for the film technique. On the basis of delayed tests which measured retained information, he showed that the experimental group averaged 38 per cent higher than the control group. Arnspiger (4) discovered that, on the basis of recall tests, the experimental groups in natural science showed superiorities ranging from 9 to 18 per cent and the experimental groups in music showed superiorities ranging from 14 to 32 per cent. On the basis of subjective observation and judgments of teachers, Consitt (9) concluded that the use of the motion-picture film in teaching elementary school children history materially aids retention. Knowlton and Tilton (22) found that photoplays contributed considerably to the gaining and retention not only of factual information but particularly of interrelationships other than time.

5. Are educational sound and silent films more effective with children of low or of high ability?

While there is evidence that films are of more benefit to the slow than the fast learner, there is reason to believe that this reflects a situation in which the technique appeals so much to the slow learner that the extreme enthusiasm with which he responds seems to the observer to be lacking among bright pupils. For this reason, subjective judgments may be misleading. Nevertheless, such investigators as Wise (35), Reitze (29), Westfall (34), Arnspiger (4), Consitt (9), and others pointed out the success with which silent and sound films are used among children of low ability. The following qualifying statement made by Hoban should, however, be borne in mind:

> Differences in the reactions of "dull" and "bright" students to films are those of degree, not of kind. Because "dull" students who frequently are not responsive to books and other verbal materials often respond quite noticeably to pictorial materials, it is sometimes said that films are better for "dull" than for "bright" students, whereas the real difference is in the kind of materials to which the response has been made, not in the kind of response to motion pictures.
>
> Because films are less abstract than words, and because "dull" students, by definition, have less abstract ability than do "bright" students, it does not follow that films are better for "dull" than for "bright" students. They serve the same essential functions of presenting visual data for observation and for interpretation.[3]

[3] Charles F. Hoban, Jr., *Focus on Learning,* American Council on Education, Committee on Motion Pictures in Education, Washington, D. C., 1942, p. 69.

Wise (35) concluded that the films were of particular value to students of the lowest ability in gaining information, and the students of the highest ability in acquiring spirit or atmosphere. Reitze (29) believed that in general an increase in intelligence means an increase in mean scores on a film comprehension test; this disagrees to some extent with the findings of earlier research. Westfall (34) stated that the superiority of the sound film was manifest particularly in the case of low-ability pupils in that they were better able to keep up with the average of the class. Arnspiger (4) reported that the talking picture made distinct contributions to the learning of pupils of below average intelligence. Consitt's agreement with this is shown by her statement (9) that backward children seemed to derive the greatest benefit from films, although certain groups of senior students apparently benefited equally.

This discussion must be qualified by saying that, while some sound films may be of greater benefit to low rather than high I.Q. groups, the content, purpose, and technique of the film make this a question which can be answered only on the basis of specific cases.

6. Do educational sound and silent films stimulate general interest?

Westfall (34), Clark (8), Consitt (9), Knowlton and Tilton (22), Freeman (16), and the Middlesex group (28) reported that the use of films in their experimental studies conclusively motivated and promoted heightened interest. According to Westfall (34), the pupils taking part in his study voted 5 to 1 for the sound film versus the silent. Clark (8) discovered that, in maintaining general interest already shown by students, sound and silent films had a slight advantage over lecture demonstrations. In stimulating new interest, the sound film had a slight advantage. Sustained attention was measured by taking a photograph of the audience immediately after it had experienced a disturbing auditory stimulus; under these circumstances, the sound film in the field of the physical sciences showed to advantage. Consitt (9) found that the films aroused interest, stimulated intellectual curiosity and imagination, gave such pleasure to children that this technique made history more meaningful to them, and, contrary to commonly held opinion, did not allow them to become mentally lazy but rather stimulated them to discussion and class participation. The investigators in the Middlesex experiment (28) were unanimous in their opinion that the sound film was of greater interest to the children than the silent film, but that both motivated the pupils considerably. Freeman (16) concluded that, because motion seems to make objects attractive, it heightens interest.

7. What effect does the use of educational silent and sound films have upon the voluntary reading done by children?

Opponents of educational films once feared that the use of motion-picture films would make learning so easy that reading would be deemphasized as a means of acquiring new information. Well-recognized authorities like Consitt (9), Knowlton and Tilton (22), and the investigators who have recently been working under the direction of the Committee on Motion Pictures in Education of the American Council on Education (1, 2, 3) demonstrated conclusively that viewing well-constructed educational motion pictures stimulates voluntary reading. The above Committee reported that student activities are heightened and increased in the direction of newspaper reading, search for general information, and participation in class and committee research. In citing the Tower Hill School study, "A School Uses Motion Pictures," and the Santa Barbara study, "Projecting Motion Pictures in the Classroom," Hoban (20) referred again and again to increased participation in the fields of reading and self-initiated research. Consitt (9) found that viewing history films increased voluntary reading. Knowlton and Tilton (22) during the course of their experiment kept a record of voluntary reading and found that the use of the films produced greater pupil participation in class discussion and stimulated pupils to read more supplementary materials.

8. What is the age beyond which educational sound and silent films can be effectively used?

Studies carried on at the elementary, high school, and college levels indicate the effective use of films. Reitze (29) discovered that second graders, when shown motion pictures adapted to their level, learned increased amounts of information. Consitt (9) concluded that for teaching history children below the age of nine derived less from films than did older children, probably because they have less background for understanding the film. She found that films are especially valuable for children above eleven years of age whose opportunities and experiences are limited.

It is difficult to determine definitely the threshold age at which the utilization of films is effective, because so much must depend upon the nature and presentation of the film and the need for this technique in ably and satisfactorily presenting the process or social situation concerned. Films adapted to the primary grades are being used effectively.

9. What is the contribution of the educational sound and silent film in terms of factual learning and of learning which effects changes in the social living of children?

Originally research concerned itself largely with the amount of factual information which accrued to the viewer of films. The many excellent data that have been accumulated leave little doubt that educational silent and sound motion-picture films contribute tremendously to the learning of factual information. However, their influence in producing ability to think and to reason and in leading the child toward socially acceptable behavior is of greater interest to the teacher and administrator.

Wise (35) discovered that the greatest gain by the experimental groups was made on tests which dealt with historical characters. His results indicated that photoplays contributed most to those phases of history which are concerned with people, causal relationships, and social and economic relations, and least to those concerned with dates and chronological order. He concluded that films are valuable in the introduction of detail, atmosphere, and background, and therefore stimulate the student's imagination and thus lead him to think critically and individually concerning the problems shown in the film. According to Consitt (9), the information gained from films helps children to make wise decisions and observations relative to social conduct, events, and modes of behavior. Wood and Freeman's summary (36) stated that experimental groups were superior to control groups in indirect or interpretive outcomes of instruction as well as in the immediate, concrete, or direct outcomes. Knowlton and Tilton (22) observed that the photoplays used with the experimental group contributed materially to the gaining and retention of knowledge, and also of interrelationships which are essential to the study of history and social problems. Using an "education" item which measured aspects of intelligent thinking on the basis of facts gained, Roulon (31) discovered that the groups who saw the general science films were superior in making intelligent judgments. Frances E. Taylor (1) interestingly described the way in which entertainment motion pictures shown outside the school led to such intense class discussions on manners and social customs that the social actions of the Mexican girls in her classes were modified. Hoban (20) summarized the role of the motion picture in the development of critical thinking as follows: "Motion pictures do not, of themselves, develop critical thinking, but they provide experiences particularly rich in opportunity and material for such development. The kind of critical thinking developed on the basis of film usage is likely to be more realistic and more functional in the lives of students than that developed on the basis of verbal experience alone."[4]

Motion pictures portray social customs, actions, and behavior so graphically and so vividly that those who see them cannot avoid being conscious observers and therefore critics. Well-constructed educational sound films in the social studies are such vivid portrayers of life in every part of the world that the information gained from them cannot help but affect the living and thinking of the children who see them. In brief, the film depicts facts so clearly that their retained impressions thereafter affect not only the critical thinking of the children but also their attitudes and actions. It is essential, then, that teachers carefully evaluate audio-visual aids before they are shown to pupils.

10. What effect does the educational sound and silent film have upon the oral response of those who view them?

The studies undertaken by the Committee on Motion Pictures in Education of the American Council on Education (3), which include "Projecting Motion Pictures in the Classroom," "Motion Pictures in a Modern Curriculum," "Students Make Motion Pictures," and "A School Uses Motion Pictures," give examples of well-motivated, purposive, and socially desirable oral response resulting from viewing well-chosen motion pictures. Consitt (9), Wise (35), and Knowlton and Tilton (22) drew attention to the great motivation given to oral discussion and response by educational motion pictures. Thus Consitt (9) found that, after seeing the history films, children felt and evidenced a strong desire to

[4] *Ibid.*, p. 93.

express opinions and describe scenes. According to Wise (35), the photoplays awakened an interest and a response which the usual mode of lesson presentation failed to arouse. Knowlton and Tilton (22) agreed that the photoplays produced more pupil participation in classroom discussion than the traditional technique brought forth.

11. How much more effective are educational sound films than educational silent motion pictures in helping students gain new information?

This question has been frequently asked from 1930 to the present. Before we discuss it, Charles Hoban's comment on it should be given: "The frequently raised question whether sound films are better than silent is much like the question whether students learn more from films than from books. It cannot be answered satisfactorily because it is not a valid question. Pictures have one role and words another. The better question is 'Does the subject shown in pictures require dialogue or sound effects, or need to be tied together, explained, or interpreted in words?'"[5]

Research by Hansen (18), which probed the effectiveness of sound film versus teacher explanation versus silent film on the same subject, revealed the value of the sound film when used in its entirety. After investigating various types of verbal accompaniment, Westfall (34) likewise concluded that the sound film in its entirety was best.

Hoban's appraisal (20) of the problem, quoted above, is still pertinent. To be handled effectively, a subject must include such environmental sounds as are necessary to portray graphically and realistically a process or a social situation. Under such conditions, the sound film will prove superior to the silent. A sound film based upon a well-arranged experiment accompanied by a lecture certainly has the advantage of being correct, delivered in logical sequence, and prop-

[5] *Ibid.*, p. 28.

erly timed and completely executed. But the folly of making every film a sound film, when in many cases sound can offer no advantage, is apparent.

12. Are educational sound and silent films more advantageous when shown to classroom-sized groups or to auditorium-sized groups?

Researches by Krasker (23), Knowlton and Tilton (22), and Hoban (20) have definitely indicated the advantage of treating classroom learning situations in the classroom and entertainment situations in the auditorium. The fact that most of the experimental research has been carried on among typical classroom groups, and that every effort has been made not to violate normal classroom situations when introducing the experimental factor—the sound or silent film—gives credibility to the claim that the classroom-sized group is preferable when showing educational films dealing with units of information normally treated in classroom-sized groups.

The following discussion will develop some psychological concepts which should be considered before any attempt to investigate experimentally effective classroom methods of using educational sound films.

Directed or Undirected Seeing

Everyone of us, whether aware of it or not, has experienced illusions of the senses; they do not always tell the truth. The eye, the ear, deceive us, and even the hand that we instinctively extend to test the evidence of our senses, has often played us false, though to speak more accurately, it is the mind and not the senses that is at fault. The senses make known but one thing, the sensations. The eye merely communicates the different shades of light or color; the hand, sensations of contact or movement. The mind interprets these sensations, draws conclusions, and with these conclusions constructs exterior objects endowed with numberless properties. . . . Yet if these automatic and rapid reasonings may be at fault, we have an illusion of the senses.[6]

All of us who have normal vision and normal hearing are receptive to sensations of color and sound. However, the distortions which our imaginations and mental processes place upon identical visual stimulations may run the gamut of the sum total of the past experiences which the individual or group may possess. Because of their greater backgrounds of experience and information, adults are often said to be poorer observers than children, for the latter's interpretations of sensory stimulation by the eye and ear are less colored by their imagination or experience because they have not lived as richly or as fully as adults.

"How can the sensations received by the ear and eye be more correctly interpreted?" is a question that underlies learning via the audio-visual route. To say that exposure to sound film stimuli affects learners equally is without foundation. Numerous parallels to support this contention can be cited. Perhaps the first psychologist to record observations relative to the distortions, fabrications, and misconceptions which individuals place on identical auditory and visual stimuli was Hugo Münsterberg. His examples of illusions— the inconsistencies which even adults of high intelligence and alleged training can display when reacting to visual stimulation in spite of having been warned to take care in drawing their conclusions—are too valuable to be omitted in any discussion of audio-visual learning. One of his experiments follows:

Last winter I made, quite by the way, a little experiment with the students of my regular psychology course in Harvard. Several hundred young men mostly between 20 and 23 took part.

[6] Alfred Binet, *The Psychology of Prestidigitation,* Annual Report of the Board of Regents of the Smithsonian Institution, Government Printing Office, Washington, D. C., July, 1894, p. 555.

It was a test of a very trivial sort. I asked them simply, without any theoretical introduction, at the beginning of an ordinary lecture to write down careful answers to a number of questions referring to that which they would see or hear. . . . At first I showed them a large sheet of white cardboard on which 50 little black squares were pasted in irregular order. I exposed it for five seconds and asked them how many black spots were on the sheet. The answers varied between 25 and 200. The answer, over 100, was more frequent than that below 50. . . . Then I showed a cardboard which contained only 20 such spots. This time the replies ran up to 70 and down to 10. We had here highly trained, careful observers, whose attention was concentrated on the material, and who had full time for quiet scrutiny. Yet in both cases there were some who believed they saw seven or eight times more points than some others saw; and yet we should be disinclined to believe in the sincerity of the two witnesses of whom one felt sure that he saw 200 persons in a hall in which the other only found 25.[7]

Possibly the argument may be advanced that this represented judgment and not observation; but what is judgment other than the working or conclusion of mental processes in an attempt to interpret or coordinate the stimuli which our senses bring to us? After being warned to observe carefully and to note conclusions, students at the college level, after being confronted with only two simple visual stimuli, made the above erroneous responses. What, then, will the naïve, carefree pupil at the elementary or high school level do when confronted by myriad, quickly passing sound and visual stimuli such as he sees in an educational sound film? What will he do later when he is asked to record his impressions as to what he observed, what he saw, and on the basis of these facts to generalize or to evaluate his behavior?

Literature, too, offers illustrations of faulty observation:

[7] Hugo Münsterberg, *On the Witness Stand*, Clark Boardman Company, Ltd., New York, 1933, p. 22.

The parson had wanted to know whether the pedlar wore ear-rings in his ears, and an impression was created that a great deal depended on the eliciting of this fact. Of course, every one who heard the question, not having any distinct image of the pedlar as *without* ear-rings, immediately had an image of him *with* ear-rings, larger or smaller, as the case might be; and the image was presently taken for a vivid recollection, so that the glazier's wife, a well-intentioned woman, not given to lying, and whose house was among the cleanest in the village, was ready to declare, as sure as ever she meant to take the sacrament the very next Christmas that was ever coming, that she had seen big ear-rings, in the shape of the young moon, in the pedlar's two ears; while Jinny Gates, the cobbler's daughter, being a more imaginative person, stated not only that she had seen them too, but that they had made her blood creep, as it did at that very moment while there she stood.[8]

That even the most astute observers are the victims of their individual mental processes is illustrated by this account:

There was, for instance, two years ago in Göttingen a meeting of a scientific association, made up of jurists, psychologists, and physicians, all, therefore, men well-trained in careful observation. Somewhere in the same street there was that evening a public festivity of the carnival. Suddenly, in the midst of the scholarly meeting, the doors open, a clown in highly coloured costume rushes in in mad excitement, and a negro with a revolver in hand follows him. In the middle of the hall first the one, then the other, shouts wild phrases; then the one falls to the ground, the other jumps on him; then a shout, and suddenly both are out of the room. The whole affair took less than 20 seconds. All were completely taken by surprise, and no one, with the exception of the president, had the slightest idea that every word and action had been rehearsed beforehand, or that photographs had been taken of the scene. It seemed most natural that the presi-

---

[8] George Eliot, *Silas Marner,* Longmans, Green & Company, New York, 1919, p. 78.

dent should beg the members to write down individually an exact report, inasmuch as he felt sure that the matter would come before the courts. Of the 40 reports handed in, there was only one whose omissions were calculated as amounting to less than 20 per cent of the characteristic acts; 14 had 20 per cent to 40 per cent of the facts omitted; 12 omitted 40 to 50 per cent, and 13 still more than 50 per cent. But besides the omissions there were only 6 among the 40 which did not contain positively wrong statements; in 24 papers up to 10 per cent of the statements were free inventions, and in 10 answers—that is, in one-fourth of the papers,—more than 10 per cent of the statements were absolutely false, in spite of the fact that they all came from scientifically trained observers.[9]

Again the question may be asked, if such a performance is true of persons skilled in careful observation, what must be our responsibility to pupils in the elementary grades and high school? What is our responsibility before we ask them to think uniformly when drawing conclusions regarding facts and generalizations based upon their visual and auditory perception when stimulated by the images and sound track of an audio-visual film? In the authors' experience, two phenomena seem to recur constantly and to stand in the way of effective learning when children observe such a film. The first is characterized by absolute invention; here there is every indication that, as the mind interprets the sensations recorded by the senses, additions and inventions creep in which are the reflection of the child's plans, environmental experiences, and interests. The second is characterized by omission of information; this possibly results when the child's attention is inadvertently fixed upon some minor detail which so enthralls him that the main purpose of the scene or series of scenes is lost. This may perhaps be com-

[9] Hugo Münsterberg, *On the Witness Stand,* Clark Boardman Company, Ltd., New York, 1933, p. 52.

pared to the situation during a stage play or motion picture when a bit role is so cleverly executed that the thread of the plot or the acting of the star is completely lost by the audience. Every teacher has had the experience of having some non-essential detail of a demonstration or illustrated description command her students' attention to the exclusion of the main point of the lesson.

An illustration of the first difficulty, namely, absolute invention, is afforded by an investigation in which students were shown the film, *Children of China*. One scene makes a point of displaying the means of plowing and cultivating the fields. After the film was shown once, the investigator asked the following question: "On the basis of what you saw in the film, what animal is used to draw the plows which the Chinese farmers use in their fields?" An analysis of 87 responses revealed that six different animals had been seen pulling the plow. In order of frequency, the following were named: horse, donkey, mule, cow, bull, and water buffalo (the correct answer). Without giving the children any cue as to the correctness of their responses, the investigator discussed this point with them. The assurance of those who insisted that horses were used was marked; for in spite of the fact that the narrator pointedly described the water buffalo as the beast of burden in China, these children really believed they had seen horses, donkeys, mules, and the other animals they had named. Here was a positive invention, a twisting of the mental processes, as the result of which both the auditory and the visual sensations presented in the film were misinterpreted.

The film, *People of Chile,* affords another example. In this film, the crops grown in the Central Valley of Chile are described as being similar to those grown in the United States, and similarities in the way the people live also are emphasized. For instance, after the scene which showed the cook preparing a meal and cleaning a vegetable served perhaps every day in the homes of American school children, this question was asked: "What familiar vegetables did you see being prepared for dinner by the cook who worked in the McKenna household?" Eight vegetables were named. Here also, the positiveness with which the children claimed to have seen these vegetables gave evidence that, in the absence of any clear perception or recollection of the scene as it occurred in the film, their own imaginations substituted images which their own experience and environment had made familiar.

The second point, the omission of information, is illustrated by the production of a recent film on the Low Countries. The motion of a windmill in the remote distance was found to distract the children's attention so completely from the main action in the foreground that the entire point of the sequence was lost. Hence the film was edited and the distraction—the distant windmill—was cut.

If the facts recorded by the senses can be thus distorted, omitted, or added to by pure invention, what is the problem faced by the teacher who attempts to use carefully, advantageously, and effectively the audio-visual materials which are rapidly being made available to her? That these problems are not restricted to the field of audio-visual learning will be apparent after consideration of the following question: If such distortions occur in the minds of children, all of whom are stimulated alike by a situation which can be as carefully controlled as the imagery and sound track of the audio-visual film, what will be the range of their interpretation, invention, and omission when they report on facts and draw conclusions based on their impressions of the printed word? In other words, if such errors creep into interpretation after the children have been exposed to the objective, clear-cut, well-planned audio-visual teaching film, what errors of interpretation will they make after reading for comprehension a paragraph, a chapter, or a book concerning a given subject? Obviously, interpretation and comprehension of written information are influenced far more by imagination, interest, invention, personal background, and experience.

The purpose of the study described in the following pages is clear cut. By which of three classroom methods can such distracting factors as imagination, invention, and omission be held to the minimum in helping children to learn via the audio-visual route? What will be the effect of forewarning them, of inducing in them a mood of more uniform anticipation, of removing barriers to the reception of new ideas by explaining difficult concepts and difficult words beforehand? Finally, what will be gained by directing their attention in advance to the more vital and meaningful visual and auditory experiences in an attempt to guide them toward the objectives which the films seek to attain and away from the non-essential details of background and correlative content?

CHAPTER II

DESCRIPTION OF THE EXPERIMENT

The Problem. This experiment compared three classroom techniques by which children can be led to acquire varying amounts of social understanding and factual information presented in the films they study. It was not the purpose to attempt to justify the use of educational sound films [1] in the classroom as an aid to learning, for this has been ably investigated by others.

The following three sound-film teaching methods were used:

1. The first teaching method asked a class to view a sound film; the group had been prepared for the presentation of this film only in the course of casual and unorganized classroom work. After seeing and hearing the film, the class answered test questions.
2. The second method asked a class:
    a. To read a brief story-like description conveying a general impression or mood prior to seeing the sound film.

---

[1] "Educational sound film" implies the following points which were inherent to the production of the 27 Britannica sound films included in this study: (1) The sound film should include environmental and interpretive sounds appropriate to the action so as to make the content of the film more realistic. (2) The visual concepts included should be those which ordinarily cannot be interpreted to the student in the classroom. (3) The sound film should interpret, by a blending of the foregoing two factors, such audio-visual concepts as will stimulate the learner's eye and ear and make it possible for him to become aware of the whole situation portrayed just as if he were actually there at the scene of action observing a segment of life in all its completeness. Evidence of these three criteria has been absent in much of the research in which the relative merits of sound film versus silent film versus the traditional teaching technique have been probed. While it is not our aim to make comparisons of techniques such as those just stated, it is our purpose to compare three methods of using educational sound films. *It should be stressed, however, that care has been taken to make sure that the experiment is based on sound motion-picture films that are valid from both the educational and the curricular point of view.*

b. To study difficult words and phrases included in the sound track.
   c. To anticipate further the content of the film by studying questions which guided the students toward large areas of information presented in the film.
   d. To view the film after the above three steps had been completed.
   e. To take a test immediately after seeing the film.
3. The third method included the above five steps and in addition asked the class to do the following things 24 hours later:
   a. To respond to a prearranged set of discussion questions.
   b. To see the film a second time.
   c. To take the test a second time immediately afterward.

These three techniques will be referred to respectively as Experimental Factor 1, Experimental Factor 2, and Experimental Factor 3. The prearranged testing instruments measured changes in pupil understanding of the film at every step throughout the experiment.

The experiment can be summarized briefly as follows:

A. Which of three teaching methods used during the showing of a given list of educational sound-films results in the greatest acquisition of factual knowledge and social understanding?

B. To what extent does the successful use of these three anticipatory techniques depend upon such factors as the child's intelligence or facility for learning, or his reading ability?

Nature of Groups Participating. The study was carried on among three classes of fourth-grade students, three classes of fifth-grade students, and three classes of sixth-grade students enrolled during the school year 1942–1943 at the Marquette Elementary School in Madison, Wisconsin. In all, a total of 264 children participated in this study, which was

DESCRIPTION OF THE EXPERIMENT

begun in October, 1942, and culminated in June, 1943. The school district in which the children live includes a well-established residential area and a relatively well-industrialized area; the economic status, and hence the background conditions, ranged from low to relatively high. Many children live in the district during the fall, winter, and spring but spend the summer in the rural communities near the city of Madison.

Selection of Groups Participating. Since it was the purpose of the investigation to determine the relative effectiveness of three methods of sound film presentation in the intermediate grades, approximately equal numbers of children in the fourth, fifth, and sixth grades were included. At the beginning of the year, the classes in each grade were equated numerically for size.[2] However, the children were not equated on the basis of criteria such as reading grade, socio-economic status, or intelligence, for this seemed unnecessary inasmuch as the rotation method was to be used.

[2] The table below shows that, while there was absence among the groups, it occurred in such a way as practically to rule itself out of consideration. Criticism may be made for not weighting the standard errors of the means on the basis of the slight fluctuations in numbers because of absence, but a few experimental trials using weighted errors revealed such a slight difference as to make weighting unnecessary.

AVERAGE PERCENTAGE OF ATTENDANCE DURING SCHOOL YEAR 1942–1943

Grade	Group	Number in Class Group	Average Percentage of Attendance
4	A	29	93.3
	B	30	94.3
	C	30	92.1
5	A	29	93.0
	B	28	92.4
	C	29	92.7
6	A	29	93.1
	B	30	95.4
	C	30	95.3

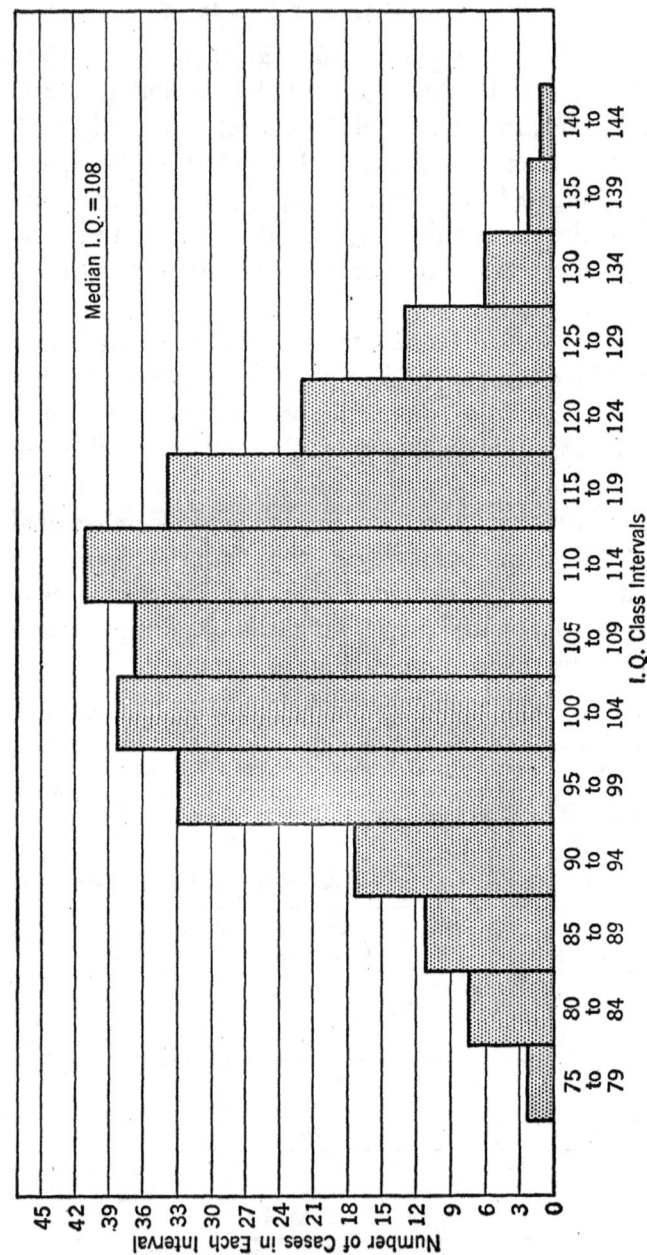

GRAPH 1. Distribution of I.Q. among 264 fourth-, fifth-, and sixth-grade children taking part in experiment; based on Pintner-Cunningham Test for Grade 4 and Kuhlmann-Anderson Test for Grades 5 and 6. Binets were given in about 10 per cent of these cases as follow-up tests; and where they were given they were used.

DESCRIPTION OF THE EXPERIMENT   33

Graph 1 shows the frequency distribution of the group on the basis of intelligence. It should be noted that the median I.Q. is 108. The distribution reflects a typical group except that the curve is slightly skewed to the right.

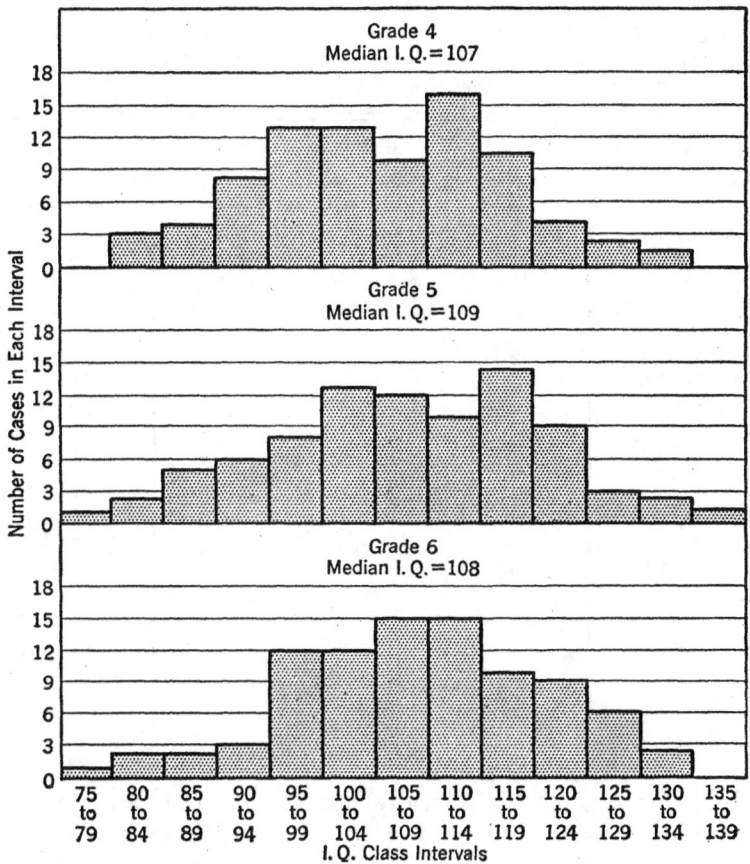

GRAPH 2. Distribution of I.Q. among children of Grades 4, 5, and 6 participating in the experiment. Distribution for each grade is shown.

Graph 2 indicates the distribution of intelligence among each of the three grades participating in the experiment.

Each of the three was normal in this respect. Thus the median for Grade 4 is 107; for Grade 5, 109; and for Grade 6, 108.

Table 1 shows the distribution of reading ability among

TABLE 1. Distribution of Reading Grades for Grades 4, 5, and 6 at Beginning of Experiment. Durrell-Sullivan Reading Test Used for Grade 4, Iowa Silent Reading Test Used for Grades 5 and 6

Reading Grade	Grade 4	Grade 5	Grade 6	Total
10.0–10.5			3	3
9.5–9.9			3	3
9.0–9.4			3	3
8.5–8.9			5	5
8.0–8.4		1	7	8
7.5–7.9		1	7	8
7.0–7.4	1	3	6	10
6.5–6.9	1	10	24	35
6.0–6.4	5	6	7	18
5.5–5.9	6	12	8	26
5.0–5.4	9	7	5	21
4.5–4.9	11	13	10	34
4.0–4.4	25	15	1	41
3.5–3.9	16	17		33
3.0–3.4	10	2		12
2.5–2.9	3			3
2.0–2.4	1			1
Total cases	88	87	89	264
Medians	4.2	4.9	6.7	

the 264 pupils. Rather typically, the children in Grade 4 vary in ability from second grade second month to seventh grade second month, with a median reading grade at fourth grade second month at the beginning of the experiment. Grade 5 shows slightly greater compactness, with ability ranging from third grade second month to seventh grade second month; however, there are fairly large groupings at the upper third- and lower fourth-grade reading accom-

DESCRIPTION OF THE EXPERIMENT

plishment levels. Grade 6 shows a wider spread of ability, with a range from fourth grade second month to tenth grade fifth month.

The reading factor enters the experiment because of the necessity of reading the questions on the examinations. The influence of this factor was held at a minimum, however, for the pupils were given sufficient time to complete their answers. Some of the pupils in the lower reading ranges were observed having difficulty with some words in the questions. While this was a handicap, it was uniform throughout the entire study and is therefore ruled out. The only effect of reading difficulty would be in the direction of lowering somewhat the accomplishment level over the entire experiment, but it would not alter the relative levels of accomplishment and therefore would not in any way change the statistical comparisons or the validity of the conclusions.

Films Used. Nine films were selected for each of the three grades on the basis of the curriculum opportunities and needs for the particular grade. In the order of screening, the films selected were as follows:

GRADE 4

1. How Nature Protects Animals
2. A People of the Congo: The Mangbetu
3. Pygmies of Africa
4. Gray Squirrel
5. Birds of Prey
6. Children of Switzerland
7. Moths
8. Pond Insects
9. The Honey Bee

GRADE 5

1. The Airplane Trip
2. Life in Old Louisiana
3. Development of Transportation
4. A Planter of Colonial Virginia
5. Arts and Crafts of Mexico
6. Pioneers of the Plains
7. Land of Mexico
8. The Truck Farmer
9. Irrigation Farming

GRADE 6

1. Children of China
2. Children of Japan
3. People of Hawaii
4. People of Mexico
5. Land of Argentina
6. People of Chile
7. Peru
8. Water Power
9. Simple Machines

These films are correlated with the various social studies and natural science units which are typically studied in the intermediate grades, and were taken from the Encyclopædia Britannica film series.

Curricular Coordination. Every effort was made to correlate the showing of the films with the social studies and natural science courses of study for the fourth, fifth, and sixth grades. For this reason it was necessary to distribute the viewing of the films according to the schedule shown below. The X's indicate the week the film was shown for each grade. For example, in Grade 6 *Children of China* was shown during the eleventh week; *Children of Japan,* the twelfth week; *People of Hawaii,* the thirteenth week, and so on. The 27 films were shown between October 1, 1942, and June 3, 1943.

	\multicolumn{27}{c	}{Week}
	1	2	3	4	5	6	7	8	9	10	11	12	13	14	15	16	17	18	19	20	21	22	23	24	25	26	27
Grade 6											×	×	×	×	×	×	×	×	×	×	×	×	×				
Grade 5	×	×	×	×	×																						
Grade 4						×	×	×	×	×														×	×	×	×

The only variable in the entire experiment was the method of anticipating the film and the use of the film. Teachers were instructed to proceed with their work in the social studies and science units as usual; normal classwork was not disrupted. Teachers who had been in the habit of using other visual aids were encouraged to continue them. The investigators were in sole charge of the class groups during the three experimental situations; the teachers often accompanied their groups but took no part.

Construction of Learning Guides. Learning guides were constructed to outline objectively the presentation methods at every step. In constructing these guides, repeated screenings of the film were made by the investigators before any story-descriptive material was written. Careful checks and rechecks of the vocabulary of the sound track and animations were made in order to set apart for pre-study the words and phrases which were unique to the development of the concepts presented in the film and essential to understanding them.

The format of the mimeographed instructions for Experimental Factors 1, 2, and 3 was kept constant. The story-description sections were held to approximately the same length in terms of reading time and word count. In each case the section, "Words and Phrases You Must Know to Understand This Film," was confined to a vocabulary which included the nouns, verbs, and phrases judged necessary to understanding the concepts. Similarly, the section, "What to Look for in This Film," contained question suggestions which anticipated the major concept areas of the films used.

Description of Test Items. Prior to the experiment, the investigators developed objective tests of fifty items for each of the 27 films. The validity of the test items was established by securing written sequences of the sound track and carefully noting the social concepts of custom, habit, living conditions, architecture, land forms, labor conditions, etc., included in the film but not mentioned in the sound track. As many as fifteen screenings of the film were often made before the investigators were completely satisfied that the tabulation of the visual concepts and the verbal sound track was accurate.

The tests included true-false questions, one-response 3-part multiple choice, one-response 4-part multiple choice, two-response 5-part multiple choice, and in some cases, where the nature of the content was thus best served, three-response 6-part multiple choice. The major portion of each test was assigned to direct recall or fill-in questions. In general, between 20 and 25 per cent of the test items consisted of true-false questions; between 25 and 30 per cent, multiple-choice questions; and about 50 per cent, direct recall. A specimen of the tests is included in Appendix A. The tests were administered in advance to subjects other than the children in the study for the purpose of removing questions which were ambiguous, too difficult, or too easy.

After reviewing many of the able researches in the field of audio-visual instruction (Arnspiger, Knowlton, Consitt, and others), the reader might well inquire why pre-tests were not used in this study. Here the type of information being sought is of importance. The above experiments were concerned with the use or non-use of films, or the use of sound versus silent films. In the present study, however, the same audio-visual materials were used with all the children in each grade; this means that the only variable which could enter and could be anticipated by a pre-test of the film content would be foreknowledge of the materials, places, facts, and processes shown in the film. Since the films were closely correlated with the curricular content at each grade and therefore a high degree of curricular validity could be assumed, the factual information in the films was encountered by the pupils for the first time at the grade-level considered and through the experiences which were meant to be taught in the social studies or science units.

Another factor which made pre-tests unnecessary was the fact that to a large extent the films chosen for the investigation dealt with fields of information, foreknowledge of any portion of which would be removed through the rotation technique because of its inherent property of so doing. Many of the basic concepts in *Pond Insects, Moths,* and *The Honey Bee*—the development of the insect from egg through larva and pupa to the adult, for example—were common to all three films. Any foreknowledge of this would be carried uniformly by a student or a group of students through all three experimental factors.

Scoring the Test. Before the tests were given, objective answer sheets were worked out and validated against the sound track and visual concepts in the film. All tests were scored by the investigators on the basis of these answer sheets. In scoring, 100 was taken as perfect, two points being assigned to each response whether it was true-false, multiple choice, or complete recall.

Typical Procedure. All the sound films were shown in an auditorium which was well adapted to the presentation of sound motion pictures. Although it could seat 200, only the front rows were occupied during any one showing. In order to reduce the environmental factors to a minimum, all showings of the several films were made there. In no case was more than one film per week per class shown during the experiment. A sound projector and a beaded glass screen were used.

The following stenographic report covering Experimental Factors 1, 2, and 3 in connection with the Britannica film entitled *Water Power* reveals how they were handled. The specimen Learning Guide in Appendix A shows the type of material used with each of the 27 films.

TYPICAL TECHNIQUE, EXPERIMENTAL FACTOR 1
(Average time, 35 minutes)

TEACHER. Today we are going to begin the study of water power. All of us have many questions as we begin our study.

Study itself will raise many others. Before we begin, we will look at this sound picture about water power and its development through the past. We will see how man used water power to do work, how the use of water power has grown in the United States and in other countries. We will see how water power is changed into another kind of power—electricity—which in turn does much of man's work today.

Lights were put out, the film was shown, and the pupils returned to their classrooms where the tests were passed out and taken. Regular classwork continued. The tests were scored by the investigators.

Typical Technique, Experimental Factor 2
(Average time, 45 minutes)

TEACHER. The film you are going to see today is entitled *Water Power*. The heading "White Coal—The Sun-given Power of Falling Water" has several meanings packed into it. Can any of you tell what the heading means?

PUPIL. It might be how the sun reflects on the water.

TEACHER. Will someone else try?

PUPIL. Water falling makes power if it is used the right way. Coal gives power, too.

TEACHER. Yes, and that is why water power is compared to it. Why is it called "white" coal?

PUPIL. The falling water looks white.

TEACHER. Why is it called "power"?

PUPIL. Water creates power.

TEACHER. In what way may it create power?

PUPIL. By making electricity.

TEACHER. Yes, who can explain how this "power" is "The SUN-GIVEN *power* of falling water"?

PUPIL. The sun draws the water up into clouds and when it rains, the water drops.

TEACHER. Yes! After water has completed its run to the sea, it

DESCRIPTION OF THE EXPERIMENT 41

is hoisted up again. What does that tell you about our supply of falling-water power?

PUPIL. It will never give out.

PUPIL. As long as we have the sun, it won't.

TEACHER. Will you now read with me the story on the front page. Read silently as I read aloud.

"A century ago Lester Pelton stood watching miners break down banks of gold-bearing gravel with powerful streams of water. 'What great force water has when under pressure!' he might have thought. 'What work water can do if properly harnessed!' And soon, he put these thoughts into action.

"For ages, man has used falling water to turn wheels—water wheels. It was less than a century ago, however, that Pelton hit upon the idea of imprisoning falling water within tubing or hose. By releasing this imprisoned falling water through a nozzle and against the cupped blades of a water wheel, great force and high speed could be attained. In the years that followed, factories near waterways of the United States clustered themselves about the foot of dams and piped falling water to their machinery in the manner Pelton had invented. One thing was wrong. Factories had to come to falling water; falling water could not be led great distances to factories.

"But soon, inventors changed that. Falling water was led to water wheels, water wheels turned newly invented electric generators, generators developed electric power, and electric power was carried to factories several hundreds of miles away. Falling water still provided the power, but in a changed form—electrical energy.

"Everywhere, where water falls in great volume, men now say—'There fall tons and tons of white coal.' What do they mean? They mean that the white, gleaming masses of water which plunge over natural falls and man-made dams the world over can be harnessed to do work. They mean that some day white coal on the Amazon, the Congo, the Ganges, and the Hoang-Ho will be doing man's work forevermore—forevermore, or as long as the sun lifts up water, and rains drop new 'white coal' upon the high lands."

Now let's read about what we are to look for in this film. Look at the section, "What to Look for in This Film."

1. "Be able to describe how the early citizens of the United States used water power." Some of you may know that already.

2. "Be able to describe how falling water is transformed into electric energy by the modern turbine and generator."

3. "Where in the United States are the largest water-power developments located?" If you have been reading the newspapers and magazines you know that now.

4. "Be able to identify the parts of the turbine and generator."

5. "By what means and over what distances can electric power be carried?"

6. "How is electric power used in the home of the average citizen?"

7. "What has the government done to help water-power development in the United States?"

8. "Where among the rivers of the world are great water-power resources available?"

9. "What European countries have led in the development of water-power resources?"

10. "Why aren't the water-power resources of the world more fully developed?"

Now, look at the third section, "Words and Phrases That You Must Know." What is meant by "artificial waterfalls"?
PUPIL. It means it is made up by man.
PUPIL. Dams are man-made waterfalls.
TEACHER. What often is the purpose of making artificial waterfalls?
PUPIL. To hold water in one place and let it fall a great distance.
TEACHER. What is meant by the phrase, "churning butter"?
PUPIL. Isn't it making butter out of milk?
PUPIL. Out of cream.

DESCRIPTION OF THE EXPERIMENT

Pupil. Doesn't it mean using the power of pushing-up-and-down? Isn't that man-made?

Teacher. The first answer was correct—making butter out of cream.

Teacher. "Electric generator"?

Pupil. In the circus, they have electric generators. In this way, they make their own electricity wherever they need it.

Teacher. Yes. Do you know how those generators are spun?

Pupil. They are all charged up.

Teacher. No. Bill was referring to generators on trucks that produce electric power. They have to have something to make the generators operate.

Pupil. I think they are run by big batteries.

Teacher. No, not by batteries.

Pupil. By gasoline engines or Diesel engines.

Teacher. Yes. Here they are converting one form of energy into another.

Pupil. Don't the farmers have a windmill with something on top?

Teacher. Yes, they turn wind power into electrical power. Who can give us a definition of an electric generator? What does it do?

Pupil. A machine that changes some other kind of power into electricity.

Teacher. Yes! What kinds of power are used to generate electricity?

Pupil. Wind.

Pupil. Water.

Pupil. Diesel.

Pupil. Steam.

Pupil. Gasoline.

Teacher. What we are going to talk about, then, is a generator which uses which kind of power?

Pupil. Falling water.

Teacher. What is meant by "Ganges River"?

Pupil. Isn't that the sacred river of India? They burn the bodies of their dead and throw the ashes into the river.

TEACHER. Yes, the Ganges River is the sacred river of India. What is a "grist mill"?
PUPIL. Isn't that a handmade mill used in olden days to grind coffee through and grain?
TEACHER. A grist mill is one usually used to grind corn, grain, or wheat. How was the machinery of the early mills turned?
PUPIL. By water.
PUPIL. By wind.
TEACHER. "Hoang-Ho" is what?
PUPIL. A river in China.
TEACHER. What is a "hydroelectric plant"?
PUPIL. A plant that uses water to make electricity.
TEACHER. Yes.
PUPIL. Don't they usually have those hydroelectric plants by the dams so they don't have to put too much work into getting water to the plant?
TEACHER. Yes.
PUPIL. Doesn't the word "hydro" stand for "water"?
TEACHER. Yes, it is a Greek word. Where is the nearest hydroelectric plant near Madison?
PUPIL. Near Merrimac.
TEACHER. Where is the "Indus River"?
PUPIL. In India.
TEACHER. Where is the "Orinoco River"?
PUPIL. In Africa.
TEACHER. No!
PUPIL. In China.
TEACHER. No! I wouldn't hire you for a guide!
PUPIL. In South America.
TEACHER. "South America" is right. What part of South America?
PUPIL. In the northern part.
TEACHER. Where is the "Paraná River"?
PUPIL. In Brazil.
TEACHER. Yes, it runs through southern Brazil and Paraná. A "penstock" is what?
PUPIL. Isn't that where they put cattle?

(*Pause.*)

TEACHER. That's a guess! We'd better go to the dictionary. The dictionary definition is, "the lead-in pipe through which water is carried from the dam to the generator." What does "turbine" mean?

PUPIL. A hat.

TEACHER. That's one meaning—a turb*an* is a hat but not this one. This word is turb*ine*.

PUPIL. A water wheel.

TEACHER. Right! But what kind of water wheel?

PUPIL. Doesn't it turn the water into electricity?

TEACHER. Yes, but who can describe it further? (*No answer.*) It is a particular type of water wheel that is enclosed. An enclosed water wheel is called a "turbine." There are two pronunciations of it: turbĭne and turbīne. Turbĭne is preferred.

TEACHER. Where is the "Yangtse-Kiang River"?

PUPIL. In China.

TEACHER. Where is the "Zambezi River"?

PUPIL. In Africa.

TEACHER. Now we shall see the film.

After the first page of materials was read and discussed, the film was shown. Immediately after the showing, the children returned to their own classroom and, still under the direction of the investigator, answered in writing the fifty questions which covered the content of the film. Later these questions were scored by the investigator.

TYPICAL TECHNIQUE, EXPERIMENTAL FACTOR 3
(Average time, 90 minutes)

[The techniques used in the first half of Experimental Factor 3 are the same as those used in Experimental Factor 2. After the children had completed Experimental Factor 2, they returned to the auditorium the following day to discuss the film. In every case the prearranged discussion questions were adhered to rigidly. A report of the responses to the questions on the same film, *Water Power,* follows.]

TEACHER. Who would like to talk about the first question?
PUPIL. "Explain in detail how water power is converted into electrical energy." First, the water is let out of the dam, and it goes down in a tunnel, and it shoots out and then the water wheel catches the water and that turns it around and there is an axle going up and that turns the turbine and then the turbines make the generators go and the generators turn the water power into electricity.
TEACHER. There is one thing you are not quite straight on.
PUPIL. The water wheel is the turbine.
TEACHER. Does the water turn the generator directly?
PUPIL. No, it turns the turbine which is on the same shaft as the generator.
TEACHER. Yes. Who would like to explain the second question: "Explain how the sun enters into the creation of water power"?
PUPIL. The sun draws the moisture from the earth, takes it up into the clouds, and when they gather, it rains.
TEACHER. You have the idea. The sun in that way redeposits water on the hills. "What source of water power is still unused by man?"
PUPIL. Waves in oceans and lakes that splash on the rocks.
TEACHER. Yes, the power of waves and . . . ?
PUPIL. Tides.
TEACHER. "Explain how the old grist mills turned water power into mechanical energy." Did they use turbines?
PUPIL. They used a water wheel only.
TEACHER. "Describe how a turbine harnesses water power," and let's add, how does a turbine harness more water power than a water wheel?
PUPIL. By turning the wheel.
TEACHER. No.
PUPIL. Because the turbine gets all the water from the river.
TEACHER. Try that again. It doesn't get *all* the water.
PUPIL. It gets most of it from the dam.
TEACHER. Why?
PUPIL. Because the water is all dammed up.

DESCRIPTION OF THE EXPERIMENT

TEACHER. What is the advantage of the turbine over the water wheel?
PUPIL. It goes faster.
TEACHER. Why?
PUPIL. It is enclosed.
TEACHER. Yes. Can any of the water escape going right past the wheels of the turbine?
CLASS. No.
PUPIL. Where does the water go after it turns the turbine?
PUPIL. Into the river below the dam.
PUPIL. Then it comes back into the turbines?
TEACHER. No. Is the turbine above or below the dam?
CLASS. Below.
TEACHER. As you see the film again, watch very carefully and follow the path of the water. Watch the arrows and the explanation and you can't help but understand how it operates. Let's go on to the next question.
PUPIL. "Where in the United States is the government now building huge projects which convert water power into electric energy? What other uses of water do these projects make available to man?" In Grand Coulee, Bonneville, Roosevelt.
PUPIL. Boulder.
PUPIL. Niagara.
PUPIL. Tennessee Valley Authority.
TEACHER. How many dams are there in the TVA?
PUPIL. Quite a few.
TEACHER. Yes, there they catch the water, use it, build another dam farther downstream, and use the water again. "Where in your state has industry taken advantage of the power which falling water releases?"
PUPIL. Chippewa Falls.
PUPIL. Sauk City.
PUPIL. Wisconsin Rapids.
TEACHER. Yes, and the Fox River is dammed at several places.
PUPIL. What about Beaver Dam?
TEACHER. Yes, and that one also.

Pupil. At Wisconsin Rapids they have a paper mill that makes paper for *Life Magazine* and they get power from the river.
Pupil. "Where over the world are vast water resources still going unused?" In Africa and South America and western Europe, India.
Pupil. In the Far East.
Pupil. China.
Pupil. Some parts of the United States.
Teacher. Take the second half: "In what part of the world is water power most effectively used?"
Pupil. It is used in Europe in Germany, Italy, and Switzerland.
Teacher. Where is it most *effectively* used?
Class. Switzerland.
Teacher. Switzerland uses how much?
Class. 75 per cent.
Teacher. As you see the film again, what are you going to look for that you missed seeing the first time?
Pupil. Check where the dams are in the United States.
Pupil. Where the water-power resources are all over the world.
Pupil. Uses in the home.
Pupil. How the dams and power machinery in the old grist mills were used.
Pupil. Parts of the turbine.
Pupil. What big rivers are just going to waste.
Etc.

Following the discussion questions, the children saw the sound film for the second time. After this, they returned to their classroom immediately and answered the fifty test questions again. Again all scoring was done by the investigators, this second response being recorded as the score for Experimental Factor 3.

The procedure with the three experimental groups may be summarized as follows:

Experimental Factor 1 anticipated the film only in the

course of the usual class situation; there was no specific or controlled anticipation of seeing the film. The film was shown and the pupils were asked to answer the test prepared for it.

Experimental Factor 2 anticipated the film; only the first page of the Learning Guides (see Appendix A) was used. The children then saw the film and took the test for it.

Experimental Factor 3 anticipated the content of the film by having the children discuss the items included on page 1 of the Learning Guides. They then saw the film and took the test prepared for it. Twenty-four hours later the children met and discussed the questions prepared in advance for the film (see Appendix A, page 4, "What to Talk About"). Following the discussion, they saw the film a second time and afterward took the same test. This test was scored and these scores were taken as the data for Experimental Factor 3.

The Statistical Technique

The rotation method of group experimentation was used in order to minimize the effect of several uncontrollable factors which must necessarily be reckoned with in any study comparable to the present one. By rotating the subjects and holding constant the various experimental factors, such variables as chronological age, emotional differences, rapport, intelligence, level of reading ability, and influence of teacher can be reduced to a common level of interference or even to nothing.

Further reasons for using the rotation method are as follows: the fact that the purpose of this experiment was to determine the amount of advantage or disadvantage due directly to three experimental factors, and that this method made it possible to reduce to a minimum the influence of earlier experiences on the children's reactions to the experimental factors. The three factors—no anticipation, half anticipation, and full anticipation—were set up on the basis of a 3-3-3 rotation. In other words, the three groups in each grade were shown three films, the three experimental factors being used; furthermore, for the purpose of assembling a large body of experimental data, the three groups in each grade went through the experience three times. Table 2 shows one rotation followed by each child in each of the three grades.

Examination of this table shows that for film A, *China,* the children in Group A (Teacher 1) saw it under Experimental Factor 1 conditions. The children in Group B (Teacher 2) saw it under Experimental Factor 2 conditions, and the children in Group C (Teacher 3) under Experimental Factor 3 conditions. This represents one cycle. When these same children viewed film B, *Japan,* the children in Group A saw this film under Experimental Factor 2 conditions, the children in Group B under Experimental Factor 3 conditions, and the children in Group C under Experimental Factor 1 conditions. When these same groups saw film C, *Hawaii,* they rotated through the third set of experimental conditions. The sum total of their experience was that each group of children saw three films, one film being viewed under each of three experimental conditions.

Suppose, for example, that the children in Group A represented an unusually bright class. This would mean that the effect of this high intelligence would reflect to the advantage of each one of the three experimental factors; in other words, its benefit would be distributed uniformly, *not to the specific advantage of any individual factor.* If Group C happened to be unusually good in reading, the advantage of this superiority would be distributed uniformly among the experimental factors. The same comment holds true in regard

TABLE 2. Summary of One Rotation for One Grade for Three Films
Summary of Rotation 1 for Grade 6 for the Three Films:
A. *China;* B. *Japan;* C. *Hawaii*
Group A (Teacher 1)   Group B (Teacher 2)   Group C (Teacher 3)

A	E.F. 1 IT^1 FT^1 C^1 24 62.45 M = 38.45 SD = 10.71 SEM = 2.33	E.F. 2 IT^1 FT^1 C^2 24 74.2 M = 50.2 SD = 8.37 SEM = 1.87	E.F. 3 IT^1 FT^1 C^3 24 89.7 M = 65.7 SD = 4.71 SEM = 1.05
B	E.F. 2 IT^2 FT^2 C^5 21 79.08 M = 58.08 SD = 6.53 SEM = 1.36	E.F. 3 IT^2 FT^2 C^6 21 88.43 M = 67.43 SD = 6.97 SEM = 1.48	E.F. 1 IT^2 FT^2 C^4 21 67.42 M = 46.42 SD = 7.42 SEM = 1.42
C	E.F. 3 IT^3 FT^3 C^9 19 84.95 M = 65.95 SD = 8.02 SEM = 1.71	E.F. 1 IT^3 FT^3 C^7 19 58.26 M = 39.26 SD = 9.26 SEM = 1.97	E.F. 2 IT^3 FT^3 C^8 19 76.84 M = 57.84 SD = 7.51 SEM = 1.5

E.F. 3−1 $(C^3+C^6+C^9)−(C^1+C^4+C^7) = (199.08)−(124.13) = \frac{74.95}{3} = 24.98$

E.F. 2−1 $(C^2+C^5+C^8)−(C^1+C^4+C^7) = (166.12)−(124.13) = \frac{41.99}{3} = 13.99$

E.F. 3−2 $(C^3+C^6+C^9)−(C^2+C^5+C^8) = (199.08)−(166.12) = \frac{32.96}{3} = 10.99$

Level of Performance E.F. 1 $(SFT^{EF1} \div 3)−(SIT^{EF1} \div 3) = (62.7)−(21.33) = 41.37$
Level of Performance E.F. 2 $(SFT^{EF2} \div 3)−(SIT^{EF2} \div 3) = (76.7)−(21.33) = 55.37$
Level of Performance E.F. 3 $(SFT^{EF3} \div 3)−(SIT^{EF3} \div 3) = (87.7)−(21.33) = 66.37$

Mean SD of E.F. 1 = $(SDM^{C1} + SDM^{C4} + SDM^{C7}) \div 3 = 9.13$
Mean SD of E.F. 2 = $(SDM^{C2} + SDM^{C5} + SDM^{C8}) \div 3 = 7.47$
Mean SD of E.F. 3 = $(SDM^{C3} + SDM^{C6} + SDM^{C9}) \div 3 = 6.57$

to any unusual, ordinarily uncontrollable variable which may enter into an experimental situation, as, for example, superior classroom environment, the development of superior or inferior study habits, poor or excellent discipline, etc.

Similarly, if the tests developed for the three films were of unequal difficulty, this inequality would be reflected uniformly as the three groups rotated through the three experimental factors and the three films. If, however, the superiority of one or two of the experimental factors had become apparent, this obviously could not be rotated out of the experiment; it would appear whenever the experimental factor was used and would be absent when it was not used.

In Table 2, the letters IT indicate the initial test score or the computed zero score of the test, the assumed or nearly pure zero point of difficulty of each test. This score was arrived at by estimating the effect of chance. The pure score or C score was determined by subtracting this chance factor from each individual score. The IT was computed so that the true levels of accomplishment for each of the three experimental factors could be established. Since there is a 50–50 or better opportunity of answering a true-false question correctly on the basis of chance, one-half the total score possible in answering true-false questions in any one test was allocated to the IT value as the correction for chance. Similar corrections were made for multiple-choice questions, but no correction was made for completion questions. In this investigation every attempt was made to hold to a minimum the element of chance in the construction, administration, and scoring of the objective tests. Thus the C scores for the three experimental factors represent as nearly as possible the true level of accomplishment for the respective groups. For each class, the mean final test score was reduced by the IT score to produce the mean C score.

The letters SD in the table indicate the standard deviation; SEM indicates the standard error of the mean.

The method of computing the comparative levels of performance is shown at the bottom of Table 2. The final test scores for each factor and for each rotation were added; the computed IT scores for these tests were subtracted from

THE STATISTICAL TECHNIQUE

this. Likewise the standard deviation of each experimental factor was computed for the purpose of investigating whether or not any trends relative to the increasing homogeneity or heterogeneity of the groups could be discerned in their accomplishment. Finally, the differences between levels of accomplishment for the three factors were computed.

The question next arises, What findings would probably result from subsequent samplings at similar or identical grade-levels among a further and unlimited population? If the type of sampling that has been used in the 27 cases covered in this study could be continued to an unlimited extent, would the means continue to show the same trend? Or is there a possibility that chance has allowed the 81 samplings to be selected so fortunately that they show the differences they do?

The statistical formula which is recommended by Fisher (14), Yule (37), Lindquist (24), and McCall (25) and which is specifically designed for handling the type of data[3] developed in this study is as follows for the data presented:

$$\frac{\text{Difference}}{\sqrt{\text{Sums of the Squares of the SEM}}}$$

(1) Significance of difference between Experimental Factors 3 — 1

$$\frac{(C^3 + C^6 + C^9) - (C^1 + C^4 + C^7)}{\sqrt{(SEM^3)^2 + (SEM^6)^2 + (SEM^9)^2 + (SEM^1)^2 + (SEM^4)^2 + (SEM^7)^2}} = \text{Standard units or critical ratio}$$

(2) Significance of difference between Experimental Factors 2 — 1

$$\frac{(C^2 + C^5 + C^8) - (C^1 + C^4 + C^7)}{\sqrt{(SEM^2)^2 + (SEM^5)^2 + (SEM^8)^2 + (SEM^1)^2 + (SEM^4)^2 + (SEM^7)^2}} = \text{Standard units or critical ratio}$$

(3) Significance of difference between Experimental Factors 3 — 2

$$\frac{(C^3 + C^6 + C^9) - (C^2 + C^5 + C^8)}{\sqrt{(SEM^3)^2 + (SEM^6)^2 + (SEM^9)^2 + (SEM^2)^2 + (SEM^5)^2 + (SEM^8)^2}} = \text{Standard units or critical ratio}$$

[3] Data which are derived from independent samplings of the same population and are based not on calculated percentages of gains or losses but rather on points.

The standard units shown above are in terms of the normal curve distribution. If a measure of three or more standard units is obtained, as has been the case in this study, it can be concluded that the differences dealt with are significant differences between the populations and that future samplings under identical conditions will display similar differences. In every case in the present investigation, the differences proved their reliability when thus tested; in only two cases were they below four standard units. Fisher recommends that, when working with class samples from 20 to 30, as is the case in this study, the following correction should be made:

$$SEM = \frac{SD}{N-1}.[4]$$

[4] For further discussion, see Lindquist (24), Fisher (14), McCall (25), and Yule and Kendall (37).

CHAPTER III

Experimental Results and Interpretation

Experimental studies in the field of visual materials have proved conclusively the advantage of such materials, properly used, as a supplement to traditional classroom techniques. The advantage of the well-constructed sound motion picture over its predecessors—the silent picture, the silent slide, the stereopticon—has also been demonstrated. What has not been definitely established is the amount of information which the child can learn from the well-constructed educational sound film when various methods—three in this case—of utilizing it are employed.

Dr. W. W. Charters threw some light on the amount of information which a child can gain from the entertainment type film when he said: "The motion picture, as such, is a potent medium of education. Children even of the early age of 8 see half the facts in the picture and remember them for a surprisingly long time."[1]

If half the content of the entertainment film is absorbed by viewers, even those as young as eight years of age, what portion of the information included in the true educational sound film can be absorbed by students of the intermediate grades? The answer to this question will be sought from among the evidence included in this chapter.

The nine pairs of tables in Appendix B record the essence of the experimental evidence gained from 9 rotations which represent the reaction of 264 children to 27 educational sound films; they also embody a consolidation based on well over 100,000 responses to test items. The first table in each pair summarizes the levels of performance attained by chil-

[1] W. W. Charters, *Motion Pictures and Youth,* The Macmillan Company, New York, 1933, p. 60.

dren of the fourth, fifth, and sixth grades after they had been shown the several films under three experimental conditions. The Level of Performance for Experimental Factors 1, 2, and 3 represents a consolidation of the children's reactions to the three films included in the rotation covered in each table. Thus their reactions when there was little or no anticipation before the film was shown are indicated as Level of Performance for Experimental Factor 1; when there was anticipation of the film and the children responded to a test, the reactions are indicated as Level of Performance for Experimental Factor 2, etc.

The second table in each pair summarizes the computations which were made to reveal the statistical significance of the differences between levels of performance. The fact that all the critical ratios or standard units are above 3.04 indicates practical certainty that the samplings used were valid and typical.[2] This indicates also that the differences or gains made are the result of the introduction of Experimental Factors 2 and 3 and of no other factors.

The complete range of the Levels of Performance for Ex-

TABLE 3. Summary of Levels of Performance Achieved by Grades 4, 5, and 6 Under Experimental Factor 1, 2, and 3 Conditions Governing the Viewing of 27 Educational Sound Films (Three Films per Rotation)

	Grade 4			Grade 5			Grade 6		
	R 1	R 2	R 3	R 1	R 2	R 3	R 1	R 2	R 3
E.F. 1	26.09	32.82	29.77	31.67	33.64	29.83	41.37	34.91	27.92
E.F. 2	32.79	41.03	45.96	38.93	41.54	47.09	55.37	52.39	44.89
E.F. 3	47.90	53.24	58.04	49.77	55.19	59.11	66.37	64.33	55.67

[2] See p. 62.

perimental Factors 1, 2, and 3, in the order of grade and rotation in each grade, is shown in Table 3.

Graphs 3, 4, and 5 illustrate more clearly the levels of performance and the films used for each grade. Graph 3 shows that the Levels of Performance for Experimental Factor 1 vary as follows: 26.09, 32.82, and 29.77. The Levels of Performance for Experimental Factor 2 show significant increases in every case, the figures being 32.79, 41.03, and 45.96. The gain of this factor for Rotation 3 is a double one. It records a continuing upward trend over the lower level for Experimental Factor 1 and at the same time shows a gain for Rotation 2. This same trend is manifest in the levels of performance in Experimental Factor 3. In every case, the differences are statistically significant and represent not only absolute but percentage gains.

Graph 6 summarizes the levels of performance for each of the rotations—three for Grade 4, three for Grade 5, and three for Grade 6. Again the data are presented in chronological sequence and by grade. Each set of three bars represents three levels of performance for one rotation. It should be remembered that each rotation includes the use of three educational sound films under three experimental situations for three groups of students. Each rotation then reflects a consolidation of nine group reactions.

What may validly be interpreted from this? First, that the introduction of the teaching techniques in the three factors is fostering increased learning on the part of the children, and second, that not only are the gains statistically significant but they increase at an increasing rate with each rotation. This indicates without doubt that there is a definite, desirable increase in the child's ability to observe more critically, in more detail, more validly, and more persistently. In short, anticipation allows him to become an increasingly skilled observer. The reader may well question: Is not this the result

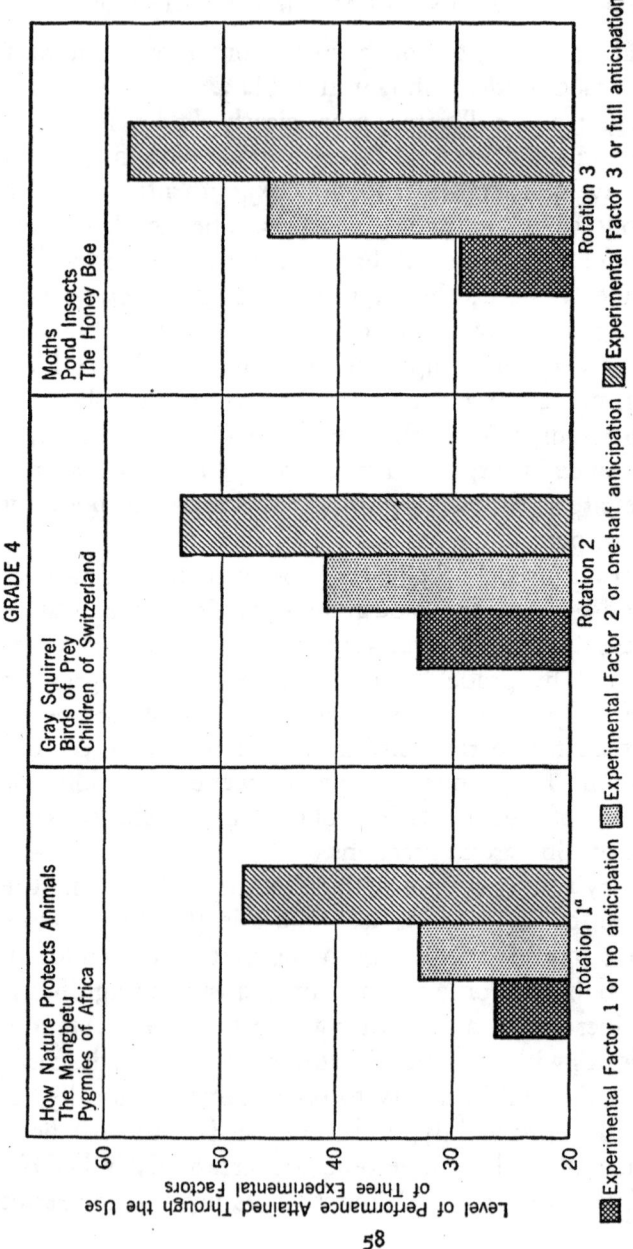

GRAPH 3. Levels of performance attained through the use of Experimental Factors 1, 2, and 3 in connection with the showing of 9 educational sound films to 88 Grade 4 children.

[a] A rotation represents the reactions of 9 class groups to 3 films under 3 experimental conditions.

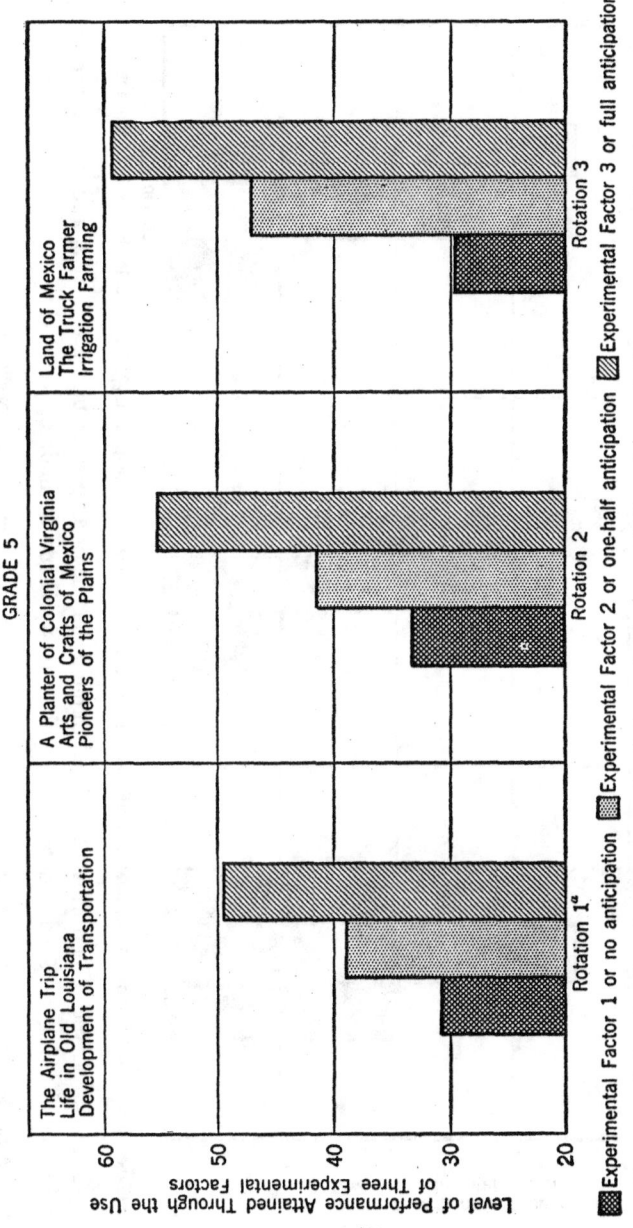

GRAPH 4. Levels of performance attained through the use of Experimental Factors 1, 2, and 3 in connection with the showing of 9 educational sound films to 87 Grade 5 children.

[a] A rotation represents the reactions of 9 class groups to 3 films under 3 experimental conditions.

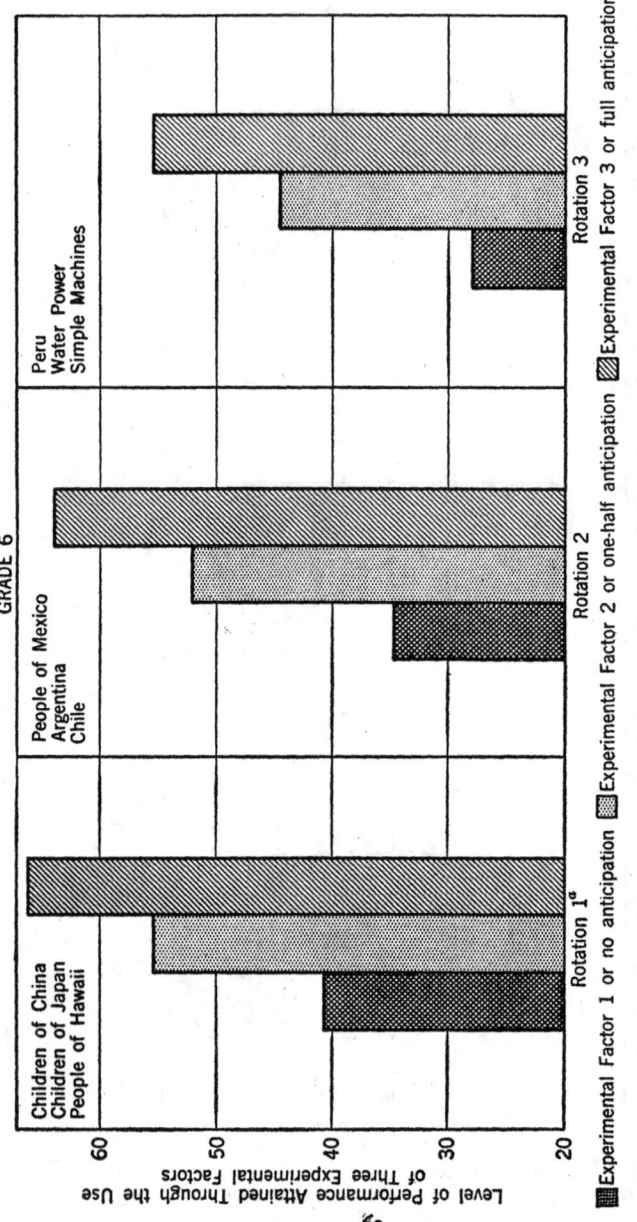

GRAPH 5. Levels of performance attained through the use of Experimental Factors 1, 2, and 3 in connection with the showing of 9 educational sound films to 89 Grade 6 children.

[a] A rotation represents the reactions of 9 class groups to 3 films under 3 experimental conditions.

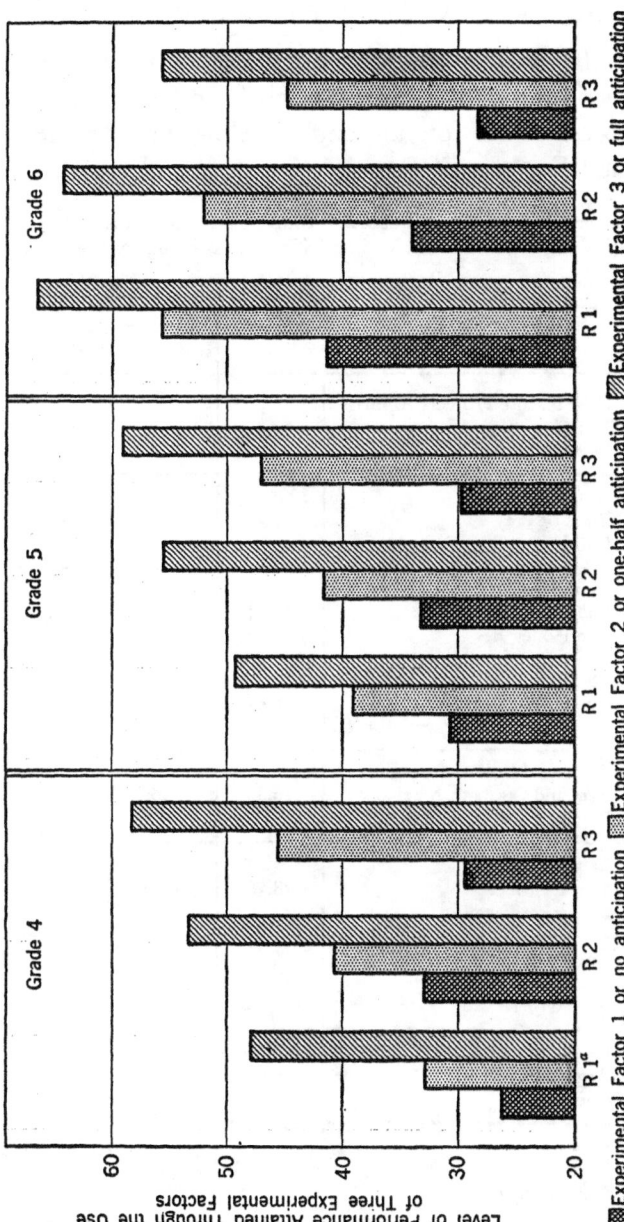

GRAPH 6. Levels of performance attained through the use of Experimental Factors 1, 2, and 3 in connection with the showing of 27 educational sound films, 9 at each grade level.

[a] A rotation represents the reactions of 9 class groups to 3 films under 3 experimental conditions.

of practice effect? The answer must definitely be negative, because practice effect would benefit all factors equally during the process of the rotation and therefore would benefit Experimental Factor 1 of Rotation 3 as well as Experimen-

TABLE 4. Summary of the Computed Standard Units or Critical Ratios as Tests of the Statistical Significance of the Various Differences Existing for the Several Films

	Film Title	Difference E.F. 3 − 1	Difference E.F. 2 − 1	Difference E.F. 3 − 2
Grade 4 Rotation 1	How Nature Protects Animals The Mangbetu Pygmies of Africa	9.9	3.04	7.16
Grade 4 Rotation 2	Gray Squirrel Birds of Prey Children of Switzerland	10.73	4.21	6.74
Grade 4 Rotation 3	Moths Pond Insects The Honey Bee	15.05	8.25	7.43
Grade 5 Rotation 1	The Airplane Trip Life in Old Louisiana Development of Transportation	9.57	3.63	5.50
Grade 5 Rotation 2	Planter of Colonial Virginia Arts and Crafts of Mexico Pioneers of the Plains	10.89	3.6	6.3
Grade 5 Rotation 3	Land of Mexico Truck Farmer Irrigation Farming	18.38	10.43	7.85
Grade 6 Rotation 1	Children of China Children of Japan People of Hawaii	17.92	9.65	8.86
Grade 6 Rotation 2	People of Mexico Argentina Chile	20.02	10.73	8.15
Grade 6 Rotation 3	Peru Water Power Simple Machines	14.52	9.25	6.65

EXPERIMENTAL RESULTS AND INTERPRETATION 63

tal Factors 2 and 3, which careful observation of Graph 6 shows is not true. Thus, it may be concluded that the upward trend in ability to observe critically and to gain increasing amounts of information is due directly to the introduction of Experimental Factors 2 and 3.

Not only are the differences or gains statistically significant, as can be seen by examining Table 4, but they represent large percentage increases. Table 5, which shows the

TABLE 5. General Trends of Improvement in Level of Performance (Relation Between New and Old Levels of Accomplishment Expressed in Percentage)

	Level of Performance of $E.F._3$ as Percentage of $E.F._1$	Level of Performance of $E.F._2$ as Percentage of $E.F._1$	Level of Performance of $E.F._3$ as Percentage of $E.F._2$
GRADE 4			
Rotation 1	183.59%	125.68%	146.08%
Rotation 2	162.22%	125.02%	129.75%
Rotation 3	194.96%	154.38%	126.28%
GRADE 5			
Rotation 1	157.15%	122.92%	127.84%
Rotation 2	164.06%	123.48%	132.86%
Rotation 3	198.29%	158.00%	125.52%
GRADE 6			
Rotation 1	160.38%	133.81%	119.85%
Rotation 2	184.24%	150.07%	122.77%
Rotation 3	199.39%	160.78%	124.01%

general trend of improvement in level of performance when each new level is computed as a percentage of the old level, indicates improvements of Experimental Factor 3 over Experimental Factor 1 ranging from 157 to 199 per cent. The level of accomplishment achieved under Experimental Factor 3 conditions in Rotation 3 for all grades is nearly double the level achieved under Experimental Factor 1 conditions. For example, the use of Experimental Factor 3 among the fourth-grade students practically doubles the amount of information secured from seeing the sound film compared to the level of performance attained when the traditional method of seeing films—with little or no anticipation—is used.

Much the same interpretations can be made for Grade 5. Here again, every recorded difference between Experimental Factors 1, 2, and 3 is validated by critical ratios or standard units of 3.04 or better (see Table 4), which indicates that it is extremely probable that the differences are significant. More than this, the levels of performance, even in the face of the decreases shown in Experimental Factor 1 for Rotations 1, 2, 3, have an upward trend which again may be considered an indication that the children are definitely increasing their ability to observe as they progress through the sequence of the experiment. Table 5 shows that, when Experimental Factor 3 is compared with Experimental Factor 1, the differences in performance vary from 157 to 199 per cent. In Rotation 3, the use of Experimental Factor 3 virtually doubles the amount of information which students gain from seeing educational sound films such as those used in the experiment. Every claim made for Grade 4 may be made for Grade 5 and is therefore more completely substantiated.

Analysis of Graph 5 covering Grade 6 reveals similar information. At first glance, the reader may be puzzled at the downward trend of the Experimental Factor 3 levels of performance. This, however, is corrected by the steeper downward trend of Experimental Factor 1 for Rotations 1, 2, and 3; this makes clear at once the increase in the differences between Experimental Factors 1 and 3. This is revealed numerically in Table 5 by a range of from 160 to 199 per cent for Rotations 1 to 3 inclusive. Again the conclusions which have been set forth for Grades 4 and 5 hold for Grade 6.

Gains Made on Specific Educational Sound Films

The observation may be made that the introduction of Experimental Factors 2 and 3 is of increasing significance as the child's familiarity with the film subject decreases. Examination of Tables 9A through 17A reveals many examples.

In the fourth grade when films such as *Gray Squirrel* and *Children of Switzerland* were viewed, gains of 19 and 15 were recorded for Experimental Factor 3 levels over Experimental Factor 1 levels. These subjects are relatively close to the experience of children of this age. However, when subjects more removed from their experience and hence representing greater difficulty as far as the assimilation of new information was concerned were introduced, the differences were larger. On such films as *The Mangbetu, Birds of Prey, Moths, Pond Insects,* and *The Honey Bee,* differences in levels of achievement for Experimental Factors 3 — 1 were as follows: 27, 27, 29, 25, 30.

Similar examples are afforded by Grade 5 experience. Differences in level of achievement for such films as *The Airplane Trip* and *Development of Transportation* were much lower than for such films as *Irrigation Farming, Land of Mexico,* and *A Planter of Colonial Virginia.* The reason again seems to be that as the child explores areas of experience which are removed from his own everyday background, he gains increasing benefits from such study assistance as Experimental Factors 2 and 3 offer.

As the child progresses through the curriculum of the elementary school he broadens his horizons and finds himself going farther afield from his community, his own neighborhood, and his home. In the sixth grade, the difficulties of the films increase and the differences in the levels of achievement likewise are greater. The differences in levels of achievement for Experimental Factors 3 — 1 for films on China, Hawaii, Argentina, and Peru are high: 27, 27, 33, 27. Likewise, when the sixth-grade children viewed the film, *Simple Machines,* the introduction of Experimental Factors 2 and 3 resulted in a gain of 30 points.

It may be concluded, then, that the introduction of Experimental Factors 2 and 3 is of increasing value to the child as he goes into the higher grades and studies film subjects which portray more abstract concepts and unfamiliar places.

Is There a Relationship Between Aptitude and the Child's Ability to Observe and Learn from Educational Sound Films?

Research has compared the information gained from motion-picture films by pupils in the upper and lower I.Q. ranges. Frances Consitt (9) believed that pupils with a low I.Q. gained more information from seeing silent pictures than did pupils with a high I.Q. Other investigators—Wise (35), Westfall (34), and Arnspiger (4)—made similar statements. The present investigators, however, feel that this finding is due largely to the casual and traditional methods of using motion pictures. Because of these methods, the pupil with a high I.Q. has not been sufficiently advised or motivated, whereas the pupil with a low I.Q. has found the novelty of the situation and the freedom from being bound by reading inadequacies such an incentive that he has shown himself a superior observer.

During the course of the investigation, subjective observation indicated the possibility that, if the more intelligent pupil were encouraged by means of anticipatory techniques such as are characteristic of Experimental Factors 2 and 3, he would do as well as and possibly better than his less in-

APTITUDE AND EDUCATIONAL SOUND FILMS 67

telligent fellow classmate. Accordingly, an analysis was made to ascertain the nature of the gains achieved by these two categories of pupils during the experiment. The reader will recall that with Experimental Factor 3 the film was anticipated and then shown, the pupil was then tested and then allowed to discuss the film, after which the film was shown again and a second test administered. The existence of two sets of test data permits the following comparison:

Points of improvement[3] in relation to I.Q. have been plotted on a scattergram (Table 6). The scattering of the population makes possible the arrangement of arrays on both axes and gives a typical picture of no correlation. Means have been computed for each array on both axes. The mean improvement for each I.Q. interval from 70 to 140 is recorded at the extreme right. Since the means in the 70 to 90 I.Q. range are based on such a limited number of cases, they may well be excluded from consideration. The remaining means vary from 11.9 to 12.7; there is no significant difference between them and therefore in all probability only a slight trend. The means for the I.Q. arrays on the vertical axis vary between 105 and 112 and reveal no significant trend either up or down. Several tests of correlation—for example, the Pearson Product-Moment Coefficient of Correlation or the analysis of variance technique—could be applied, but there is obviously no use in doing so.

The following conclusions, therefore, can be made regarding the relationship between point gains of improvement and I.Q. level:

1. All I.Q. groups are capable of making comparable gains in the information obtained as the result of seeing the sound films viewed under Experimental Factor 3 conditions.

---

[3] Points gained = last half of Experimental Factor 3 test results — first half of Experimental Factor 3 test results.

TABLE 6. Points of Improvement in Relation to I.Q. When Individual Pupil Scores of Improvement Are Plotted. These data are taken only from Experimental Factor 3 Differences in first and second test scores.

I.Q. Range	-2	0	2	4	6	8	10	12	14	16	18	20	22	24	26	28	30	32	34	36	38	40	42	44	46	48	50	Mean Points of Improvements in Each Array
140+					1																							
130				4	2	3	2	1	1	1	1		4															12.5
120			1	9	13	16	15	12	10	3	12	4	4															12.4
110		5	6	14	21	37	31	29	21	15	10	8	5	4	3		1	1		1								11.9
100		5	3	20	29	20	32	26	22	19	13	14	13	5	4		1			1								12.6
90	1	3	7	5	14	13	14	14	19	8	11	8	1		1		1	1										12.7
80		1		1	1	6	11	7	4	4	6	4	2			1	1		1									15.8 (fewer cases)
70									2																			17.6
Mean I.Q. for Each Array		105	106	112	108	109	109	107	107	105	108	110	105	110	109													

Points of Improvement (E.F. 3 − E.F. 2) for Individual Cases

2. There is a slight trend in the direction of slightly larger gains being made by low than by high I.Q.'s, but this trend is apparent only in a few cases among the groups with the lowest I.Q.'s.

3. The distribution shows conclusively that the pupils with high I.Q.'s were not restrained from further learning by any "ceiling" or barrier.

4. The distribution shows that, contrary to the findings of earlier studies, pupils with high I.Q.'s can, with proper motivation and direction, use audio-visual materials as effectively and beneficially as pupils with low I.Q.'s, if Experimental Factor 3 conditions may be used as the criterion.

5. If this population is typical of others, children with low I.Q.'s are capable of improvement comparable to that of pupils with high I.Q.'s, and vice versa, providing that proper classroom methods of motivation, anticipation, discussion, and testing, similar to those in the learning guides, are used.

Correlation Between Reading Grade and Test Scores

The Pearson Product-Moment test for correlation was applied to one-third of the total 81 series of scores. Nine series for each grade, or 27 series in all, were chosen from the fourth, fifth, and sixth grades so as to represent a sampling of the grades, of the A, B, and C groups for each grade, and of the three experimental factors used with each grade. The method of selection was as follows: For Experimental Factor 1, three series representing performance of Groups A, B, and C in Grade 5 on Films 13, 14, and 15, and three series representing performance of Groups A, B, and C in Grade 6 on Films 25, 26, and 27 were used to test for possible correlation between reading grade and test scores. A similar procedure was followed for Experimental Factors 2 and 3.

In Table 7 in the column headed "Per Cent" are tabulated the squares of *r;* they have been computed because they show the percentage of the deviations which can be associated with reading grade. For example, for Film 1 and Experimental Factor 1, r equals .56, and its square, 31%, indicates the percentage of deviations that can be associated with reading grade. From this it follows that the other 69% of the deviations cannot be associated with reading grade. The other percentages in Table 7 are to be interpreted similarly. The following conclusions may be made from the data in this table:

1. A correlation does exist between reading grade and test scores. The degree to which deviations are influenced by reading grade varies widely, from 1 to 79 per cent.

2. Experimental Factor 2 correlations are lowest; Experimental Factor 3 correlations are next, and Experimental Factor 1 correlations are highest. This may be interpreted as indicating that reading is a measure of intelligence and that the best readers have the widest background of information for Experimental Factor 1.

3. As the experimental factors are introduced, the influence of reading grade, and possibly also of the intelligence that this grade implies, decreases. This is evidenced by decreasing measures of correlation.

4. Correlations tend to decrease from grade to grade, being lowest in the sixth grade. This implies either that more information is obtained through the film itself, that the influence of reading grade is less, or that reading grade is less important as a measure of background information.

5. Correlations tend to decrease as the difficulty of the film increases. On the basis of the Level of Performance for Experimental Factor 1, the films *Land of Argentina, People of Chile, Water Power,* and *Simple Machines* are more difficult. Likewise the percentages of deviation associated with reading grade are lowest. This may reasonably be taken as

TABLE 7. Sampling Correlations for Each Group for Each Film and for Each Grade to Test Correlation Between Reading Ability as Measured at the Beginning of the Year and Reactions to Films as Measured by the Learning Guide Tests in Experimental Factors 1, 2, and 3

SAMPLING FOR GRADE 4

Film	Group	E.F. 1		E.F. 2		E.F. 3	
		r	Per Cent	r	Per Cent	r	Per Cent
1. How Nature Protects Animals	A	.56	31				
2. The Mangbetu	B	.79	62				
3. Pygmies of Africa	C	.80	64				
4. Gray Squirrel	C			.58	33		
5. Birds of Prey	A			.64	40		
6. Children of Switzerland	B			.68	46		
7. Moths	B					.89	79
8. Pond Insects	C					.45	20
9. The Honey Bee	A					.63	39
			Ave. 52		Ave. 39		Ave. 46

SAMPLING FOR GRADE 5

10. The Airplane Trip	A					.63	39
11. Life in Old Louisiana	B					.80	64
12. Development of Transportation	C					.58	33
13. A Planter of Colonial Virginia	C	.73	53				
14. Arts and Crafts of Mexico	A	.80	64				
15. Pioneers of the Plains	B	.82	67				
16. Land of Mexico	B			.64	40		
17. The Truck Farmer	C			.53	28		
18. Irrigation Farming	A			.03	1		
			Ave. 61		Ave. 23		Ave. 45

SAMPLING FOR GRADE 6

19. Children of China	A			.70	49		
20. Children of Japan	B			.45	20		
21. People of Hawaii	C			.16	2.5		
22. People of Mexico	A					.47	22
23. Land of Argentina	B					.35	12
24. People of Chile	C					.40	16
25. Peru	A	.68	46				
26. Water Power	B	.42	17				
27. Simple Machines	C	.32	10				
			Ave. 24		Ave. 24		Ave. 17
Average of Total			Ave. 46		Ave. 29		Ave. 36

an indication that as film subjects become more difficult, reading grade decreases in significance. Under these same circumstances the introduction of Experimental Factors 2 and 3 is of the greatest importance; that is, the effectiveness of these two factors, mainly the third, increases as the difficulty of the films increases. In other words, as the films become increasingly difficult, the necessity for properly anticipating the viewing of these films likewise increases.

Homogeneity of the Groups Increased by the Use of Experimental Factors 2 and 3

As the children went through the experiment, it became apparent that the performance of the nine class groups clustered increasingly about the means as the experimental factors were introduced. The evidence presented in Table 8 in terms of the standard deviations of the scores made by the nine groups under Experimental Factor 2 and 3 conditions shows that the introduction of these factors creates increasing homogeneity in the groups' performance. In other words, in the face of improved levels of performance secured through the introduction of Experimental Factors 2 and 3, the standard deviations decrease slightly and reveal greater compactness. This is significant because normal progress in learning usually produces increasing heterogeneity. Thus the use of the Learning Guides produces increases in performance among the slow learners which balance the increases made by the fast learners.

Summary

1. In every case and for each of the three grades, the level of performance attained through the method of presentation referred to as Experimental Factor 3 reveals

SUMMARY

TABLE 8. Standard Deviations for 3 Rotations and for 3 Grades to Show Decreasing Tendencies Which Indicate Increased Group Homogeneity During the Experiment

	Rotation 1			Rotation 2			Rotation 3			Total
	E.F. 1	E.F. 2	E.F. 3	E.F. 1	E.F. 2	E.F. 3	E.F. 1	E.F. 2	E.F. 3	
Grade 4	13.86	11.55	12.38	12.24	10.85	9.81	13.10	10.41	9.25	E.F. 1 = 39.2 E.F. 2 = 32.8 E.F. 3 = 31.4
Grade 5	11.22	12.25	9.97	12.33	14.02	12.01	10.50	9.56	8.5	E.F. 1 = 33.9 E.F. 2 = 35.8 E.F. 3 = 30.4
Grade 6	9.13	7.47	6.57	9.77	9.78	7.87	12.85	9.34	10.38	E.F. 1 = 31.7 E.F. 2 = 26.5 E.F. 3 = 24.8

improvements which are virtually double those attained through the classroom technique described as Experimental Factor 1.

2. In Rotation 3, after properly anticipating, viewing, discussing, and reviewing the educational sound films, the children who participated in this study practically doubled the amount of information gained from the 27 films in comparison with the children with whom Experimental Factor 3 was not used.

3. In every case substantial gains are shown in the levels of performance attained through the use of the three experimental factors, and in every case these gains are statistically significant. However, even during the final weeks of the experiment, the levels of achievement failed to indicate complete mastery of the content of the films.

4. It is interesting that in Rotation 3 the achievement levels for all grades with Experimental Factor 2, which we

may call 50 per cent anticipation, show gains which are very close to 50 per cent of improvement. Likewise Experimental Factor 3, which may be called 100 per cent anticipation, enables gains which represent virtually a 100 per cent improvement over the levels achieved with Experimental Factor 1. No additional anticipation could produce as efficient results.

5. The statistical evidence shows conclusively that, through the use of Experimental Factors 2 and 3, children become increasingly able observers; that is, they increase their ability both to observe factual information and to use this information in answering test questions which proved their ability to make social judgments not specifically identified with the film itself or with the sound track.

6. As the films become more difficult (the difficulty based on the Level of Performance for Experimental Factor 1, which is particularly outstanding in Rotations 2 and 3 for Grade 6), the introduction of Experimental Factors 2 and 3 increasingly affects the level of performance in a positive direction. In brief, the more difficult the film, the more effective becomes the anticipation provided for by Experimental Factors 2 and 3.

7. Children with a low and those with a high I.Q. seem to be motivated equally and to learn to a comparable degree from educational sound films. Contrary to the findings of earlier studies, when children of high ability are confronted by material similar to the Learning Guides used in this study, they show as great ability to gain information as do children of lower intellectual status.

8. Reading grade is correlated with level of performance as measured by the pupils' reactions to the tests on the experimental factors. The correlations vary widely from 1 to 79 per cent; in other words, reading ability may influence performance by any amount between these two ranges. The

SUMMARY

correlations tend to decrease as the grade increases—they are higher in Grade 4 than in Grade 6—and as the difficulty of the film increases.

9. The introduction of Experimental Factors 2 and 3 tends to produce an increased group homogeneity. This is revealed by a slight decrease in the standard deviations of the test score series during the experiment.

CHAPTER IV

Pupil Reactions to Sound Films

Why do we attend motion pictures by the tens of millions each month? Why are we so eager to push half dollars through the ticket-seller's window for the opportunity of watching fiction, biography, current events, and news in a series of alternating lights and shadows? Is it because of our love of literature or our love of adventure? Or is it because of our inherent wish to find a means of escape from the realities that so ruthlessly press us?

According to psychologists, we love comic strips because they give us an opportunity for self-inflation when we see the ridiculous antics of the characters; or we may secretly identify ourselves with the hero and his romantic deeds. Similarly, the entertainment film provides release, an opportunity to identify ourselves with heroic action and adventure and to escape care for a few brief hours of association with dreams, unfulfilled ambitions, and heroic acts. That adults are not the only ones addicted to the entertainment film is evidenced conclusively by the studies sponsored by the Payne Fund and substantiated again and again by psychiatrists, physicians, and social workers.

It has been already established that the entertainment film was the first to make and leave an impression upon 130,000,000 Americans. Hence it is not unlikely that the school child will be somewhat taken aback when, after being told that a motion picture will be shown, he is shown not technicolor, adventure, and dazzling heroines, but an 8-minute black-and-white sound film, *How to Avoid Catching Cold*. The conscientious teacher thus has to face an initial barrier raised before the receptive thinking of the child who has been brought up on the perpetual emotion of the western thriller. The children she teaches have the idea that a movie means entertainment, relaxation, freedom from work, and a Saturday afternoon in the dusky interior of the downtown theater. To such a child it may make no difference that an educational sound film is a vitalized threshold to learning, learning which heretofore has been delimited and even inhibited by the inflexible format of textbooks, pen-and-ink drawings, and descriptions laboriously "written down" by college professors. It may make no difference to him that his eyes are seeing 24 frames of pictures each second, that 1440 of these frames are blending themselves each minute to make up the motion he is witnessing. He may not realize that through the medium of the 14,400 separate pictures which constitute a 10-minute sound picture, the doors of a textbook-bound geography are being opened and new vistas brought to him in all their reality, with all their environmental sounds, in an effort to give him a picture of life as it actually exists in the far-off Congo, on the steppes of Russia, on the rocky shores of the Aleutians, or in the paddy fields of Japan.

At the beginning of the year this barrier was apparent among the children who participated in the sound-film experiment described herein. At the onset they were keenly disappointed when, instead of an entertainment theme, the motion picture presented a unit of information close to what they were studying in their social studies work. Inasmuch as the investigators made every attempt to establish a rapport that would make the pupils feel free to be absolutely frank in their criticism or approval, the reaction of the minority to a test on the film content was not unexpected. They felt that work, or a test, had no place in anything pertaining to the movies. To these children, who had been in the habit of seeing only entertainment films, anything presented by motion pictures was to be looked at, enjoyed, discussed briefly, imitated for some time in the neighborhood, and then forgotten.

For example, one film on Africa showed what the people look like and where they live and how the animals, trees, and flowers of the region look; it also showed the process of constructing a home, securing food, bartering with neighbors, weird head decorations, and native dances and music—concepts which heretofore were often learned incompletely through the medium of the printed word. Seeing sound films and obtaining from them information formerly less adequately treated as a part of class work was so strange to most of the children that many at first refused to accept the innovation. They failed to see the analogy between this new technique and the old—reading 20 to 30 pages in a social studies book over a period of four or five days, discussing the content of these pages, being tested on their interpretation of it, and developing projects based on ideas and information gained from this reading. However, repeated explanation of the fact that the learning experience was the same except that the material was learned by means of a sound film led to increasing acceptance. Once they understood this, their comments revealed that each film was accepted more and more by them as another source of information that is clear, full of new information, and fascinating.

That their original impressions were gradually dispelled is evidenced by such pupil comments as the following:

Sound movies made it easier for me to understand about things. They don't use such big words as the geography book does.

Seeing the films gave me new and different ideas.

I learned from the films how countries really look, how people look. I got a better idea of what part of the world the country was at.

I never knew how some of the people lived when I read in books and I didn't know what kind of clothes they wore or how they looked.

It's fun and interesting because it tells what books don't tell. It makes it more plain to me. I can really see things.

Such comments show that the children realize that sound films provide an opportunity to make use of a new medium which presents old and new information to them vividly and in real-life situations, and allows every child to experience hearing and seeing to the same degree.

This last point was particularly evident among the children who had less imagination, poorer reading ability, and little experience with things or ideas beyond their immediate environment. Such comments as the above upheld the contention that asking children to interpret the printed word on the basis of their own background of experience gives rise to countless misinterpretations and miscomprehensions. In comparison, consider the opportunity which the educational sound film provides—it makes it possible to present an audio-visual image which, largely independent of imagination and background, offers a complete story comprising factual information in its own background or setting.

In illustration of this point: After sitting in on a class discussion of the characteristics of a delta region, one of the investigators asked for oral descriptions of a delta. Some of the children thought that a delta was congested with shrubbery and that low, rolling hills rose on the horizon. Others thought that it was a place with bayous bordered by tall shade trees, and with clear and sparkling water. Some saw rapids and current; others, sluggish, muddy water. Obviously each child was thinking of a delta in terms of his previous visual experience. On the basis of their past ideas of landscape, water, forest growth, and farming, the children had developed their concept of a delta. Contrast to this the discussion after the children had viewed typical delta country as portrayed in a sound film. They have had a new experience, have received living and moving auditory and visual impressions. They have gained these impressions through the sound of a voice which each child has heard similarly and through images on the screen which the children have viewed uniformly, at least as far as the film as a whole is concerned. Naturally, there are individual differences in ability to assimilate detail and in breadth of past experience; nevertheless, each child has seen the same image, the same action, the same processes, and each child has these as a foundation upon which to base his new interpretations.

It is this oneness of experience that puts children with diverse backgrounds and varying abilities in a position to respond. It is largely because of this factor that in subsequent class discussions the children hold a somewhat equal position of authority and recollection concerning the content of a sound film. It is because of this that the slow child can supplement or correct, with a high degree of self-confidence, the impressions or observations of even the brightest child in the class. Witnessing a sound film produces a common denominator of new information which naturally is seized upon by children and used equally by dull and bright.

It should be borne in mind, however, that seeing films correctly is exacting work. For the learner to master effectively the maximum content is anything but easy. But it is work that is probably more generously rewarded, on the basis of effort made and benefit received, than are other traditional classroom techniques of learning. This point may be illustrated by citing an analysis of the concepts per page in one well-known fourth-grade geography that has recently been published. The purpose of this discussion is not to criticize the book, which handles the subject very effectively, but to bring out the difference in the spacing and in the rapidity with which the children using that book are expected to acquire new concepts. The chapter on the Congo River Basin takes up 20 pages, with about 10 concepts, or basic ideas, per page. In short, somewhere between 175 and 200 concepts are included in this 20-page chapter.

In the normal classroom, anywhere from two weeks to a month is spent on this one chapter. Not all of this time, naturally, is devoted to searching for information; a great deal of it is given to class discussions and projects. However, the type of information in this chapter closely approximates the information presented in a 10-minute educational sound film on this same area, in which 124 concepts [1] are developed. The average fourth-grade child will read the 20 pages in the book with comprehension during several class periods. It would be preposterous to claim that a child could come into the classroom, see this film, and in ten minutes gain the same amount of information as is developed methodically in the 20 pages. On the other hand, consider the reaction of a classroom teacher who was told: "Here is a sound film which you can show in ten minutes. Show this repeatedly during several class periods or for about the same length of time the children would spend in reading about this same information." Obviously no right-thinking teacher would do this. But how many of us are content with showing a sound film once and then sending it back immediately to the central bureau. To repeat, seeing educational sound films is work. They must be planned. They must be anticipated. The information obtained must be tested. Classroom discussion is a necessity and reshowings of the film must be provided for. Showing an educational sound film once is comparable to spending ten minutes reading the paragraph headings in the geography textbook, then putting the book away, content that the work has been covered. As much time can be spent on an educational sound film as is spent in com-

---

[1] A study of the educational sound films used in our experimental research reveals that the number of concepts per film ranges from 47 to 130. Most of the films present between 80 and 110 concepts per 10-minute reel of 400 feet.

prehending a chapter of a good textbook. To believe that one showing of a sound film provides an effective educational experience is a fallacy of which too many of us are guilty. Using educational sound films is work, just as using wisely a chapter in a textbook is work. It demands preparation, anticipation, discussion, rereading, and attention to points which are not clear. Without all of these, no well-informed teacher would attempt to achieve valid learning and desirable social habits among the children she teaches.

Elementary and junior high school pupils certainly do not have the background of personal experience clearly to understand environmental characteristics, social problems, and cultural patterns as they actually exist. Much of our casual teaching discusses social problems sketchily and incompletely in the attempt to mold acceptable patterns of behavior among our children. However, in the film on Brazil, when pupils see children of their own age or younger working from dawn until dusk in the coffee field, when they see that only the overseers' children attend school, when they see the wretched and filthy shacks of the laborers contrasted with the ultra-modern architecture of Rio de Janeiro, when they see the meager entertainment facilities available to children and adults of the working class, they experience the nearest thing to actually living what they see. The vividness of the environmental sounds and settings and the emotional and physical response of Brazilian youngsters who strain untiringly at sorting endless quantities of dusty coffee beans gives children a background against which to discuss such social problems as universal education, housing standards, and child labor laws.

During the experiment, the children's responses were noted and summarized on the basis of type and frequency. The greatest interest was evidenced in seeing how other people live, how backward or how amazingly up-to-date other people are as they live and work and play. This included their language, their homes, their clothes, their transportation, their religious customs, and their eating habits. Such comments as the following are typical of others in this category:

I thought that the Chinese and the Japanese wore robes. Instead many wear clothes like ours. Their cities are modern like ours.

I learned how to pronounce some foreign words. I heard how they talked in Brazil and in Japan. I could see what people made.

In Hawaii I always thought there wasn't any civilization or any cities.

The films changed my ideas about clothing and dancing of the people in Hawaii.

I never thought Japan was so modern.

I didn't know cities in Argentina were modern like the United States.

I noticed the way the Chinese keep everything so neat and they use every bit of land.

I thought the South American countries were more backward.

I had some ideas about Hawaii such as beautiful girls with long wavy hair. I've changed them.

In the *Land of Mexico* I expected to see the people dancing and lying in the sun all the time, but I was surprised to see them a very industrious people.

I found out how the pioneers on the prairies made their houses. They made them of sod.

Most of this information could be secured during other class experiences. However, these comments indicate the impact which excursions into reality via educational sound films make upon the children's minds. In many cases children are allowed to gain only half-truths from studying a subject; and the unreality they attach to people, traditions, and customs of other lands is often apparent. After seeing the film on the pygmies of Africa, one youngster expressed real surprise that there actually were such people. Yes, he had read about them and heard stories about them, but he'd never really believed them. In view of the fact that many of the people who write books or articles on life in the Congo or the pygmies of Africa have no firsthand information themselves, it is not strange that their descriptions and impressions are often unreal or inadequate. Too much information taught in the classroom today is based on a cursory description of a museum exhibit or some traveler's impressions and hence fails to represent adequately the nature of the people, their industries and trade, their clothing and speech, their children's education, their religion and entertainment—all of which the educational sound film records accurately and completely.

Another field of interest concerned the speed and clarity of the visual image. That the pupils were impressed by the number of concepts which flashed before them during such a brief period of time, usually eight or ten minutes, is evidenced by the following typical comment:

When you read you have to see imaginary pictures, but when you see a movie you can see everything because people move around right in front of you.

What happens when thirty imaginations are turned loose in an attempt to interpret the same printed description is a challenge to many traditional classroom methods. Thus another child reported:

I like learning this way because when you see things in pictures you understand them better. When you see it with your own eyes you know it better.

A comment such as the next may throw some light upon the controversy concerning the difficulty of the spoken word of the commentator versus the printed word:

They [sound films] do not use too big words and that is good because some people cannot read very well. Sound films are so interesting because more people can get good out of them than out of books and also you see pretty scenes that you would not see in books.

As has already been indicated, reading ability correlates with ability to gain information from sound films. The preceding comment, which was made by a child who had been having difficulty with reading, is one of many which brings out the value of the spoken commentary in overcoming the difficulty inherent in the difference between one's reading vocabulary and one's oral vocabulary.

Another group of comments touches upon the vividness with which geographic location is fixed in the child's thinking as he viewed the educational sound film.

I thought that the South Pole was warm and the North Pole cold but I found that they are both cold. In Chile the south part is cold and the north part is warm.

I get a better picture of the location of the country when I see films because I see the people and learn about their way of living.

Other comments revealed interest in the education and pastimes of children of other lands. The pupils were somewhat dismayed at finding that many of the games these children play are just like their own. Their frequent questions about Mexican and Brazilian children reflected concern over their not having as much time to play as American children do. Such comments as these are typical:

I'm glad I can go to school. I wouldn't want to trade places with the children who must work in the coffee fields in Brazil.

In Japan it showed them playing games that we play. Some of them were checkers, rope jumping, and swimming.

I didn't know that the Chinese children had to learn to write with paint and brush.

The Japanese and Chinese children play games just like we do.

I learned that the Chinese have thousands of characters in their writing.

The little Mexican children have to work from sunrise to sunset.

Such comments make it clear that many children pay little attention to how children of other countries really live. So much of their thinking about other lands is associated with vague generalities that until they actually "see" foreign children playing, working, and living there is little reality.

Particularly interesting are some of the comments, such as the following, on how vividly processes are explained:

In irrigating land I thought that they used water from any lake or river close to them, but I didn't know they had to pay for it or that sometimes they had to get it from a place a hundred miles away.

The fact that water for irrigation frequently has to be brought from great distances to where it is used and that it has to be paid for is confusing to children who live where water is abundant. "I always thought that in building an adobe house they just piled clay or dirt together," was a typical comment after the child had seen the craftsmanlike way in which clay, water, and straw are mixed prior to being formed, dried, and used in building a house.

The children's reactions to the technique embodying anticipating the films may be described as completing the transition from antipathy to sincere realization that, in order to do a good job of seeing a film, preparation is just as important as for any classroom research project. Comments which at first implied boredom and asked nothing but that the projector be started and the film get under way, slowly gave place to comments which asked that showing the film be delayed until directions concerning viewing it were entirely clear. The children were quick to realize the necessity of careful observation, and during the discussion that followed the showing of the film differences of opinion frequently arose that resulted in suggestions that the film be shown again. The transition from the "entertainment attitude" to an appreciation that an educational film is an excellent means of acquiring supplementary information was apparent in many cases as early as three or four weeks after the experiment began.

Such comments as the following reflect the children's opinions regarding anticipating the showing of the film. The "it" refers to either the story or introductory setting which the children read before seeing the picture, the directions entitled "What to Look For in This Film," or "Words and Phrases You Must Know to Understand This Film."

> When I know what to look for, it helps me answer questions about the film.
>
> It helped me because it told us what to look for. I saw things that I might not have noticed. We talked about words before seeing the film. This helped me understand better what the speaker said and I could learn more.
>
> If the words were not explained to me, I would not have understood the movie as well. Studying the words was a great help.
>
> Reading the story about the film gives you ideas of what to look for.
>
> We could see it [the film] more plainly when we talked about it and we knew more about what to look for.
>
> It helped me to know what to look for in the film. When I

first started I thought it was hard but as I got on I began to think it was lots of fun because when I see a thing I remember it.

During the experiment, the thinking and the attitudes of the children were checked by asking them such questions as: "Why do you like this way of learning about things?" "What did you learn from these films that your reading had not told you?" "Did seeing the films change your ideas about anything?" "In what way was the first page of the Learning Guide a help to you?" "How did taking the test on the inside pages of the Learning Guide help you?" Responses to these questions are given for one typical group which took part in the experiment. Arranged on the basis of the child's I.Q., they interpret to some degree the thinking of thirty sixth-grade pupils. Errors in spelling have been corrected, but the original construction has been retained.

Case 1—I.Q. 135; reading score 9.6.

I liked the sound films because they are a new way of learning, and a movie gives more information than just reading. . . . Films tell more about certain subjects such as the meals, clothes, work, homes of people in other countries. . . . The learning guides taught me new words. . . . The test helped me to remember the film.

Case 2—I.Q. 134; reading score 10.8.

Sound films teach you to be alert and help you to find out things without a lot of reading. . . . In films we learn about houses and household affairs of other people. . . . I learned about a turbine and how it works. . . . The learning guides taught me new words and cleared up some history facts for me. . . . The test helped me to watch for details in the movies and to remember what I saw.

Case 3—I.Q. 129; reading score 11.3.

Learning from sound films is very interesting and gives definite ideas on the subject. . . . My ideas of Japan were changed by the film. . . . I did not think Japan was so modern. . . . The film is more interesting after I learn a little about it and what to look for from the learning guide. . . . The test brought out the main points of the film.

Case 4—I.Q. 126; reading score 7.5.

I learned about crops in different countries from the films. . . . I thought the Chinese were a backward people until I saw the film. . . . The first page of the learning guide helped me to pronounce words better and to know something about the film before we saw it. . . . The test taught me to pay more attention to details in the film.

Case 5—I.Q. 124; reading score 9.0.

I liked the sound films because they taught me important facts about other countries that I had not found in books. . . . I learned about Chinese and Mexican customs that I did not know before. . . . The learning guide helped me with the meanings of words. . . . The test made me think and summarize the film like a story. It taught me to think over what I had just seen.

Case 6—I.Q. 123; reading score 8.0.

The films showed that cities in other countries are almost the same as those in the United States. . . . I had thought the Chinese still kept most of their ancient customs until I saw the film. . . . The learning guide helped me to understand the film better. . . . The test helped me to listen more carefully and think about what I saw.

Case 7—I.Q. 121; reading score 7.6.

I liked learning from the films because I remember almost everything I see while I forget half of what I read. . . . The films of other countries showed the daily life of the common people. . . . The learning guide helped me by showing what to look for and what certain words mean. The short story about the country to be shown in the film also helped me. Without the words I would not have known the meaning of some of the sentences. . . . The test helps me to remember things.

Case 8—I.Q. 118; reading score 7.3.

I like the sound films because I could see what things look like and hear somebody telling about them. . . . The film changed my ideas about the clothing and dances of the people in Hawaii. . . . The first page made it easier to understand the film and to pronounce the words and know what they meant.

Case 9—I.Q. 118; reading score 7.5.

The sound films are more up-to-date and tell more about actual happenings. . . . I learned how the Chinese write with paint and brush and have many things the same as in the United States. . . . The first page helped me to find what to look for. . . . The test helped me to remember what I saw in the film.

Case 10—I.Q. 117; reading score 8.4.

I like the sound films because they give important facts about other countries, the people and their customs. . . . I learned about the six simple machines and how they are used. . . . The films changed my ideas about the Chinese and their habits. . . . The first page was a guide to me for the things to look for carefully. . . . The test helped me to look carefully at the films.

Case 11—I.Q. 115; reading score 11.6.

The sound films are a more interesting way of learning and not as dull as books. Things seem more lifelike and real. . . . The films show large cities, homes, industries, and many other things that you can read about but not see. . . . The films changed my ideas about the people and their way of living in Mexico. . . . The first page was a great help to me. . . . It mentioned the things to look for, helped me to pronounce words. The little introduction was interesting. . . . The test helped me to remember the important facts.

Case 12—I.Q. 114; reading score 7.6.

I like the sound films because I get more out of what I can really see. . . . I learned about the homes, food, and people in other countries; how machines work; how water power makes electricity. . . . I learned that the Chinese and Japanese children play some of the same games that we do. . . . I learned words and their meanings. The introduction made it easier for me to remember the film. . . . The test made me want to know more about the film and helped me to remember more about it.

Case 13—I.Q. 114; reading score 7.8.

I like this way of learning because the pictures make it very interesting and help me with the test. . . . I learned that it is easier to take the test after seeing the film than by reading about it. . . . The first page told me what to look for and how to pronounce words and know their meanings. . . . The test is a review of the film and helped me to remember what I saw.

Case 14—I.Q. 113; reading score 7.6.

The sound films make me want to listen and learn all I possibly can. . . . The film on Argentina was interesting because it showed the way meat is prepared and taken care of. . . . The films changed my ideas about water power and Boulder Dam. The first page tells what words I should listen for in the film and that I should try to find a better definition for them.

Case 15—I.Q. 112; reading score 12.0.

The sound films tell you about different things you have not read about and help you to understand more than reading does. . . . I learned about some strange foreign customs that I had never heard or read about. . . . I learned how different families live in other countries, especially in Mexico. . . . The first page helped by telling me what to look for, some words to find meanings for, and a story of earlier happenings. . . . The test made me more alert and made me watch more carefully.

Case 16—I.Q. 111; reading score 5.9.

I like this way of learning because we get more out of the picture and we learn more. . . . I learned things that I had not read about. The films were a great help and I learned a lot from them. . . . The films changed my ideas about China and simple machines. . . . The first page helped a lot in answering the questions. The test helped me to remember more of the movie because when I read over the questions, they brought back to my mind what I saw in the movie.

Case 17—I.Q. 106; reading score 8.6.

It is easier to learn a thing when you can see it in a film. . . . The film tells what is going on at the same time that we are seeing it. . . . The first page helped by telling me what to look for. It also helped in the test. . . . The test made me look at the picture with more interest.

Case 18—I.Q. 105; reading score 8.2.

This way of learning shows the way things are done which made it easier to understand the subject. . . . The films tell what kind of houses people have in other countries. It is hard to understand what houses, land, or people look like in books. . . . The films changed my ideas about the buildings that the Mexicans live in. The first page helped me know what the film was about and helped me to understand some of the words in the film. . . . The tests helped me to be alert.

Case 19—I.Q. 103; reading score 7.7.

I like this way of learning because I learn more about different countries than if I had read about them in books. . . . The films told me about lifting things with pulleys and changed my ideas about an inclined plane. . . . The first page of the learning guide helped me to look for words and how to pronounce them. It also helped by telling parts of the story. . . . The test helped me to remember things. I watched more carefully the next time.

Case 20—I.Q. 102; reading score 9.0.

I like this way of learning better than reading because I can see the pictures and can tell better what the people look like. . . . From these films I learned that China is not as backward as I thought. . . . The learning guides helped with the pronunciation of words and their meanings. It also told a little about the film. . . . I looked at the film more closely because I knew we might get a test and in that way I got more out of it.

PUPIL REACTIONS TO SOUND FILMS

Case 21—I.Q. 102; reading score 6.2.

I like this way of learning because I get to see actually some of the things people do. . . . From these films I learned what people in other countries eat and how they build their houses. . . . Seeing the films changed my ideas about the customs, scenery, clothing, and homes in other countries. . . . The learning guide told what to look for and also told a little about the country. It helped me to look for certain things in the picture. . . . The test helped me to remember what I saw in the picture.

Case 22—I.Q. 102; reading score 7.5.

I like this way of learning because the film shows how things are really done in life. . . . The learning guide helped me to look for points in the film. . . . The tests helped me to remember what I have already seen in the film.

Case 23—I.Q. 101; reading score 5.7.

This way of learning tells more than books do. When I see things, it is more interesting. . . . I learned what children in other countries wear. . . . Taking the test helped me to look more carefully when I saw the film.

Case 24—I.Q. 99; reading score 5.2.

I liked this way of learning because I saw how people lived and do things which makes it more interesting. . . . The films changed my ideas about the dress of the people of Hawaii. . . . The test helped me to learn more than by just reading.

Case 25—I.Q. 96; reading score 5.7.

I get more out of seeing the films than I do reading a book on different countries. The films changed my ideas about the power of water. . . . The first page of the learning guide helped by telling me what to look for and giving an introduction to the country to be seen.

Case 26—I.Q. 96; reading score 7.1.

I learned about the customs of people in other countries, their dress, and dances. The learning guide taught me some new words. . . . The test helped me because I watched more carefully.

Case 27—I.Q. 96; reading score 5.3.

I liked this way of learning because I get more information than by reading a book. . . . I learned about the force of water, the simple machines, and how important the screw is. . . . I learned that China is just as modern as we are. The learning guide helped me with the meanings of words that we would hear in the film. . . . The test helped me to remember some of the things I saw in the film.

Case 28—I.Q. 95; reading score 5.9.

I like this way of learning because I get information that I would not be able to find in books. . . . I learned about the people and their work in other countries. . . . My ideas about the people in other countries being old-fashioned were changed. . . . The learning guide helped me get an idea of what the film was about and helped with some of the words that I could not pronounce or did not know what they meant. . . . Taking the test on the film helped me learn more about the other countries and made me be more careful in watching the next time we had a film.

Case 29—I.Q. 89; reading score 4.8.

I like this way of learning because it tells more than books do. . . . I learned about the people of other countries. . . . The learning guide helped by telling a little about the film. It helped me with the words, too.

Case 30—I.Q. 85; reading score 5.7.

I like this way of learning because I can see all the details. . . . In books there are only words and I can't see much of a background. In films I can hear the people and see their clothes. . . . The films changed my ideas especially about China and Japan. In Japan they have many modern inventions. . . . After I read the story in the learning guide I knew what to watch for. I looked for the new words in the movie and in that way found out what they meant. . . . The test helped me with the most important facts.

The pupil comments represent the subjective evaluation of the use of the educational sound film in the classroom. They reveal the children's acceptance of such films as a worth-while adjunct to classroom materials and techniques. But more than this, these comments, together with the statistical evidence cited in Chapter III, indicate the need for subjecting the method of using educational sound films in the classroom to scrutiny and evaluation. Like good books, maps, and other effective learning materials, good sound films must be used in a manner which will fully anticipate their value to the pupil. To use them casually is to waste a primary learning source and to deprive pupils of experience that can be gained otherwise only by living. Using the films correctly, anticipating vocabulary, setting the pace through question helps, testing for understanding, discussing, reshowing a film, and retesting will reveal to students information about processes, places, things, and social experiences in a manner yet unsurpassed by any other classroom learning technique.

CHAPTER V

SUMMARY OF THE ENTIRE INVESTIGATION

The present study compared three methods of using educational sound films in the classroom to discover:

1. Which of three techniques used in showing 27 films results in the greatest acquisition of factual knowledge and social understanding.

2. To what extent intelligence and reading ability influence the child's ability to gain information from educational sound films.

The three techniques, called respectively Experimental Factors 1, 2, and 3, are as follows:

1. The child viewed the film after having anticipated seeing it only casually during regular classroom work, and immediately afterward took a 50-item test.

2. The child read a brief story-like "setting" that described the general nature of the film, studied words and phrases necessary to understand the sound track, read questions which anticipated the major fields of information covered, viewed the film, and immediately answered a 50-item test.

3. After doing the preceding step, the child 24 hours later orally discussed a prearranged set of questions based on the film, saw the film again, and immediately took the same test again.

Twenty-seven educational sound pictures were used—nine films each for Grades 4, 5, and 6. The Grade 4 films were: *How Nature Protects Animals, The Mangbetu, Pygmies of Africa, Gray Squirrel, Birds of Prey, Children of Switzerland, Moths, Pond Insects, The Honey Bee.* Those for Grade 5 were: *The Airplane Trip, Life in Old Louisiana, Development of Transportation, A Planter of Colonial Virginia, Arts*

SUMMARY OF THE ENTIRE INVESTIGATION

and Crafts of Mexico, Pioneers of the Plains, Land of Mexico, The Truck Farmer, Irrigation Farming. The following were used for Grade 6: *Children of China, Children of Japan, People of Hawaii, People of Mexico, Argentina, Chile, Peru, Water Power, Simple Machines.* The films were selected on the basis of the social studies and natural science units studied in the course of regular class work in these three grades. Every effort was made to avoid interfering with normal class work, the audio-visual materials being treated as supplementary to the regular classroom routine.

The experiment was begun in October, 1942, and was concluded in June, 1943. The participants were 264 children drawn in equal numbers from the three grades. In intelligence the distribution was skewed slightly to the right, but reading ability was typical.

During the experiment, nine groups—three groups per grade—viewed nine films at each grade level. Each group was rotated through the three experimental factors three times in the process of seeing the nine films. The rotating group method was used in order to remove any factors other than those inherent in Experimental Factors 1, 2, and 3.

The average time spent by groups working under Experimental Factor 1 conditions was 35 minutes per film; that for Experimental Factor 2 was 45 minutes; and that for Experimental Factor 3 was 90 minutes. The various groups came to the school auditorium to discuss and view the films, returning immediately afterward to their classrooms to take the tests.

Learning Guides, uniform in format, were constructed so that the three experimental factors could be held more constant. Page 1 of each guide contained a story-introduction to the film, a section "What to Look For in the Film," and a section "Words and Phrases You Must Know to Understand the Film." Pages 2 and 3 contained an objective 50-item test based on the facts and social situations presented in the film. Page 4 contained discussion questions based on the film.

Final results were based on test scores earned on the 27 tests. Differences between class averages on Experimental Factors 1, 2, and 3 were computed. Standard units of error or critical ratios were also computed, and correlations between test scores and reading grade and between intelligence and reading grade were computed. During the experiment subjective records of student comment and reactions were taken.

On the basis of statistical analysis and subjective pupil comments, the following conclusions have been drawn:

1. In every case and for each of the three grades, the level of performance attained through the method of presentation referred to as Experimental Factor 3 reveals improvements which are virtually double those attained through the classroom technique described as Experimental Factor 1.

2. In Rotation 3, after properly anticipating, viewing, discussing, and reviewing the educational sound films, the children who participated in this study practically doubled the amount of information gained from the 27 films, in comparison with the children with whom Experimental Factor 3 was not used.

3. In every case substantial gains are shown in the levels of performance attained through the use of the three experimental factors, and in every case these gains are statistically significant. However, even during the final weeks of the experiment, the levels of achievement failed to indicate complete mastery of the content of the films.

4. In Rotation 3 the achievement levels for all grades with Experimental Factor 2, which we may call 50 per cent anticipation, show gains which are very close to 50 per cent of improvement. Likewise Experimental Factor 3, which may be called 100 per cent anticipation, enables gains which represent virtually a 100 per cent improvement over the levels

SUMMARY OF THE ENTIRE INVESTIGATION

achieved with Experimental Factor 1. No additional anticipation could produce as efficient results.

5. Through the use of Experimental Factors 2 and 3, children become increasingly able observers; that is, they increase their ability both to observe factual information and to use this information in answering test questions which probed their ability to make social judgments not specifically identified with the film itself or with the sound track.

6. As the films become more difficult (the difficulty based on the Level of Performance for Experimental Factor 1, which is particularly outstanding in Rotations 2 and 3 for Grade 6), the use of Experimental Factors 2 and 3 increasingly affects the levels of performance in a positive direction. In brief, the more difficult the film, the more effective becomes the anticipation provided for by Experimental Factors 2 and 3.

7. Children with a low I.Q. and those with a high I.Q. seem to be motivated equally and to learn to a comparable degree from educational sound films. Contrary to the findings of earlier studies, when children of high ability are confronted by material similar to the Learning Guides used in this study, they show as great ability to gain information as do children of lower intellectual status.

8. Reading grade is correlated with level of performance as measured by the pupils' reactions to the tests on the experimental factors. The correlations vary widely and show that on various films reading ability may influence performance from 1 to 79 per cent. The correlations tend to decrease as the grade increases—they are higher in Grade 4 than in Grade 6—and as the difficulty of the film increases.

9. The introduction of Experimental Factors 2 and 3 tends to produce an increased group homogeneity. This is revealed by a slight decrease in the standard deviations of the test score series during the experiment.

10. Entertainment films had conditioned children so that

they regarded movies as fun and relaxation, not work. Gradually, this feeling was replaced by the realization that educational sound films constitute an interesting, effective, understandable method of learning about new ideas, processes, modes of living, and social customs.

11. The children's primary interest in motion pictures concerns how other people live, work, and dress, and their social customs; and how children of foreign countries work, play, and go to school.

12. The children are highly impressed by the clarity, vividness, and speed with which the films present new material and new concepts.

13. The children not only like to learn via motion pictures, but find that the Learning Guides make the process more interesting, easier, and more lasting.

14. All the evidence—both subjective (pupil response) and objective (statistical analysis of scores)—establishes the value of adequate anticipation with educational sound motion pictures.

LITERATURE CITED

1. American Council on Education, *Motion Pictures in the Modern Curriculum,* Report of the Committee on Motion Pictures in Education, Washington, 1941.
2. American Council on Education, *Projecting Motion Pictures in the Classroom,* Report of the Committee on Motion Pictures in Education, Washington, 1940.
3. American Council on Education, *The School Uses Motion Pictures,* Series 2—Motion Pictures in Education, Washington, 1940.
4. Arnspiger, V. C., *Measuring the Effectiveness of Sound Pictures as Teaching Aids,* Teachers College Contributions to Education No. 505, New York, 1933.
5. Binet, Alfred, *The Psychology of Prestidigitation,* Annual Report of the Board of Regents of the Smithsonian Institution, Government Printing Office, Washington, 1894.
6. Brunstetter, M. R., *How to Use the Educational Sound Film,* University of Chicago Press, Chicago, 1937.
7. Charters, W. W., *Motion Pictures and Youth,* The Macmillan Company, New York, 1933.
8. Clark, C. C., *Sound Motion Pictures as an Aid in Classroom Teaching,* Doctor's thesis, New York University, 1932.
9. Consitt, Frances, *The Value of Films in History Teaching,* G. Bell and Sons, Ltd., London, 1931.
10. Dale, Edgar, *Children's Attendance at Motion Pictures,* The Macmillan Company, New York, 1935.
11. Eichel, Charles G., "An Experiment to Determine the Most Effective Method of Teaching Current History," *Journal of Experimental Education,* 9:37–40 (1940).
12. Eliot, George, *Silas Marner,* Longmans, Green & Company, New York, 1919.
13. Ellis, Don Carlos, and Thornborough, Laura, *Motion Pictures in Education,* The Thomas Y. Crowell Company, New York, 1923.

14. Fisher, R. A., *Statistical Methods for Research Workers,* G. E. Stechert & Company, New York, 1941.
15. Franklin, Harold B., *Sound Motion Pictures,* Doubleday, Doran & Company, Inc., New York, 1930.
16. Freeman, F. N., *Visual Education,* University of Chicago Press, Chicago, 1924.
17. Goodman, David, "The Comparative Effectiveness of Pictorial Teaching Materials," *The Educational Screen,* 2:358–359, 371 (1942).
18. Hansen, J. E., "The Effect of Educational Motion Pictures upon the Retention of Informational Learning," *Journal of Experimental Education,* 2:1–4 (1933).
19. Hansen, J. E., "The Verbal Accompaniment of the Educational Film—The Recorded Voice versus the Voice of the Classroom Teacher," *Journal of Experimental Education,* 5:1–6 (1936).
20. Hoban, Charles F., *Focus on Learning,* American Council on Education, Committee on Motion Pictures in Education, Washington, 1942.
21. Hollis, A. P., *Motion Pictures for Instruction,* D. Appleton-Century Company, Inc., New York, 1926.
22. Knowlton, D. C., and Tilton, J. W., *Motion Pictures in History Teaching,* Yale University Press, New Haven, 1929.
23. Krasker, Abraham, "A Critical Analysis of the Use of Motion Pictures by Two Methods," *The Educational Screen,* 20:303–313 (1941).
24. Lindquist, E. F., *A First Course in Statistics,* Houghton Mifflin Company, Boston, 1938.
25. McCall, William A., *How to Experiment in Education,* The Macmillan Company, New York, 1923.
26. McKown, Harry C., and Roberts, Alvin B., *Audio-Visual Aids to Instruction,* McGraw-Hill Book Company, Inc., New York, 1940.
27. Münsterberg, Hugo, *On the Witness Stand,* Clark Boardman Company, Ltd., New York, 1933.
28. National Union of Teachers, Psychological and Educational

Research Committee, *The Sound Film in School*, Schoolmaster Publishing Co., London, 1931.
29. Reitze, Arnold W., "The Relationship of Acquiring Information or Knowledge Obtained from Certain Educational Motion-Picture Films to the Intelligence, Grade, Age, Sex and Type of Educational Training of the Pupils," *The Educational Screen*, 17:122 (1938).
30. Rotha, Paul, *The Film Till Now*, Jonathan Cape, London, 1930.
31. Roulon, P. J., *The Sound Motion Picture in Science Teaching*, Harvard Studies in Education, Vol. 20, Harvard University Press, Cambridge, 1933.
32. Sumstine, D. R., "A Comparative Study of Visual Instruction in the High School," *School and Society*, 7:235-238 (1918).
33. Weber, J. J., *Comparative Effectiveness of Some Visual Aids in Seventh Grade Instruction*, Educational Screen, Inc., Chicago, 1922.
34. Westfall, L. H., *A Study of Verbal Accompaniments to Educational Motion Pictures*, Teachers College Contributions to Education No. 617, New York, 1934.
35. Wise, H. A., *Motion Pictures as an Aid in Teaching American History*, Yale University Press, New Haven, 1939.
36. Wood, B. D., and Freeman, F. N., *Motion Pictures in the Classroom*, Houghton Mifflin Company, Boston, 1929.
37. Yule, George Udny, and Kendall, M. G., *An Introduction to the Theory of Statistics*, J. B. Lippincott Co., London, 1940.

APPENDIX A

Learning Guide Used with Experimental
Factors 2 and 3

....
         (Name)   (Score)

For Use With
WATER POWER
(An Erpi Classroom Film)

STUDY THIS PAGE before seeing this film.

White Coal—The Sun-given Power of Falling Water.

A century ago Lester Pelton stood watching miners break down banks of gold-bearing gravel with powerful streams of water. "What great force water has when under pressure!" he might have thought. "What work water can do if properly harnessed!" And soon, he put these thoughts into action.

For ages, man has used falling water to turn wheels—water wheels. It was less than a century ago, however, that Pelton hit upon the idea of imprisoning falling water within tubing or hose. By releasing this imprisoned falling water through a nozzle and against the cupped blades of a water wheel, great force and high speed could be attained. In the years that followed, factories near waterways of the United States clustered themselves about the foot of dams and piped falling water to their machinery in the manner Pelton had invented. One thing was wrong. Factories had to come to falling water; falling water could not be led great distances to factories.

But soon, inventors changed that. Falling water was led to water wheels, water wheels turned newly invented electric generators, generators developed electric power, and electric power was carried to factories several hundreds of miles away. Falling water still provided the power, but in a changed form—electrical energy.

Everywhere, where water falls in great volume, men now say —"There fall tons and tons of white coal." What do they mean? They mean that the white, gleaming masses of water which plunge over natural falls and man-made dams the world over can be harnessed to do work. They mean that some day white coal on the Amazon, the Congo, the Ganges, and the Hoang-Ho will be doing man's work forevermore—forevermore, or as long as the sun lifts up water, and rains drop new "white coal" upon the high lands.

What to Look For in This Film:
1. Be able to describe how the early citizens of the United States used water power.
2. Be able to describe how falling water is transformed into electric energy by the modern turbine and generator.
3. Where in the United States are the largest water-power developments located?
4. Be able to identify the parts of the turbine and generator.
5. By what means and over what distances can electric power be carried?
6. How is electric power used in the homes of the average citizen?
7. What has the government done to help water-power development in the United States?
8. Where among the rivers of the world are great water-power resources available?
9. What European countries have led in the development of water-power resources?
10. Why are not the water-power resources of the world more fully developed?

Words and Phrases You Must Know to Understand This Film:

The following words and phrases should be understood before seeing the film. It may be necessary to discuss these words and phrases or to look them up in a dictionary or textbook.

artificial waterfalls	Hoang-Ho River	penstock
churning butter	hydroelectric plant	turbine
electric generator	Indus River	Yangtse-Kiang River
Ganges River	Orinoco River	Zambezi River
grist mill	Paraná River	

(NOW SEE THE FILM. Do not look at page 2, 3, or 4 until after you have seen the film.)

APPENDIX A

TEST YOURSELF

on what you saw and heard in the film.

To indicate the correct answer, draw a line under it, check it, or fill in the blank with the right word or words.

1. Water which falls as rain and rushes from high ground to low is a never-ending source of power.   TRUE   FALSE
2. According to the film, long before man realized that falling water had power, he used flowing water as: (a) a means of transportation; (b) a means of irrigating his fields; (c) a source of drinking water; (d) a place for hunting and fishing.
3. Long centuries ago, man discovered the value of waterfalls and rapids, and knew that rushing water had power.
   TRUE   FALSE

Because the first white people who came to America did not always find waterfalls where they could use the power of falling water, they built (4) .... on small streams and thus created man-made (5) ....

6. The machine which was placed in the path of falling water so that power could be got from it was called a ....
7. According to what you observed in the film, in early America water power was first used to turn machinery which: (a) pumped water; (b) ground grain; (c) ran power looms; (d) operated canal locks.
8. The grist-mill pond which you observed in the film was held back by a dam which was constructed of: (a) rock and masonry; (b) a ridge of earth; (c) wooden piles and boards; (d) poured concrete.
9. The gears and other parts of early water machinery were made out of ....
10. Water was used to turn the wheels of the machinery of the early mills either by running over the top of wheels or along the side of wheels.   TRUE   FALSE
11. So well did these early mills use water power that most of them are still in operation today.   TRUE   FALSE

12. A new source of power, steam, was developed during the .... century.
13. In order to develop steam power, ... was required as fuel to heat the furnaces, and each year millions of tons of this fuel were burned in the factories.
14. Most of the large factories which used steam power developed along the eastern coast of the United States.
   TRUE FALSE
15. Because during recent years man has been using up most natural resources at a rapid pace, he is again turning to the waterfall as a source of power.   TRUE FALSE
16. An immense source of power is available as water from the .... Lakes plunges over Niagara Falls.
17. At the base of Niagara Falls is a power plant which turns
18. the force of .... water into electrical energy. This kind of plant is called: (a) a generating plant; (b) an electric plant; (c) a hydroelectric plant; (d) a steam electric plant.

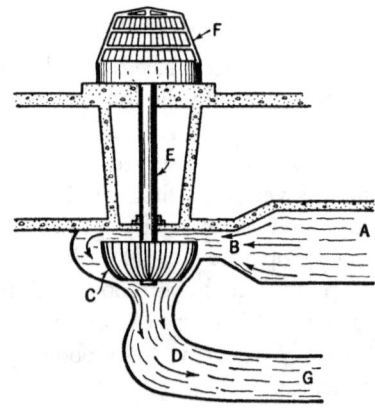

FIGURE 1.

Figure 1 shows how falling water is used to turn the machinery which changes water power into electric energy. Match the names of the parts of the machine shown in Figure 1 with the correct letters on Figure 1.

APPENDIX A

Name of parts of the machine	*Write in letters from Figure 1*
19. Electric generator	....
20. Turbine paddles	....
21. Outlet valves	....
22. Turbine generator shaft	....
23. Inlet valves	....

24. A turbine may be described as a .... enclosed in a metal case.
25. Electric current is carried over distances as long as: (a) 10 miles; (b) 100 miles; (c) several hundred miles; (d) a thousand miles; (e) several thousand miles.
26. Electric current from the power plants is carried across the country by wires which are strung: (a) along wooden poles; (b) through underground conduits; (c) from metal towers.

The Age of Electric Power has modernized many household tasks such as (27) .... and (28) ....

29. The government has developed great water-power plants partly because of its desire to provide cheap electricity to ....
30. Among the great power plants which the government has
31. developed is Boulder Dam which holds back the water of the .... River with a dam which is about: (a) 200 feet high; (b) 500 feet high; (c) 700 feet high; (d) 1000 feet high; (e) 1500 feet high.
32. Boulder Dam provides electricity to California and .... other states. In addition to providing electric power, Boulder Dam furnishes water for (33) .... and (34) .... purposes.
35. As shown in the film, other government electric projects
36. are located at (select 3): (a) Tennessee Valley; (b) Erie
37. waterways; (c) upper Ohio River; (d) Grand Coulee; (e) Bonneville; (f) Elephant Butte; (g) Shoshone Valley.
38. Vast water-power reserves are available in almost all parts

of the world. Many of them are going to waste because of lack of development. TRUE FALSE
39. Water power in the United States is much more intensively developed than it is in Europe. TRUE FALSE
40. Switzerland, which has great water-power resources, has developed about .... per cent of its water power.
41. In Europe, another country which has developed its water-power resources almost as successfully as Switzerland is ....
42. The most important things which stand in the way of
43. developing water-power resources over the entire world are (select 2): (a) a shortage of skilled labor; (b) the impossibility of sending electric power more than a few hundred miles; (c) periodic floods and drought in certain areas; (d) the difficulty of bringing supplies to some water-power sources; (e) many native peoples do not use mechanical energy.
44. A great source of water power which has as yet not been used by man is the power of the ....

Figure 2 shows some of the rivers of the world which have been or can be developed into water-power projects. Write the names of the river water-power sources after the letters listed below.

45. *South America*
46. (Write in two.)

A. ....
B. ....
C. ....

47. *Africa*
48. (Write in two.)

D. ....
E. ....
F. ....

49. *The Far East*
50. (Write in two.)

G. ....
H. ....
I. ....

J. ....
K. ....

APPENDIX A   113

FIGURE 2.

OTHER INTERESTING THINGS TO TALK ABOUT, AND DO

After looking at the film and answering the questions, you will enjoy discussion, activities, and reading of references, and you will surely want to see the film, *Water Power,* again.

WHAT TO TALK ABOUT:

1. Explain in detail how water power is converted into electrical energy.
2. Explain how the sun enters into the creation of water power.
3. What source of water power is still unused by man?
4. Explain how the old grist mills turned water power into mechanical energy.
5. Describe how a turbine harnesses water power.
6. Where in the United States is the government now building huge projects which convert water power into electric energy? What other uses of water do these projects make available to man?
7. Where in your state has industry taken advantage of the power which falling water releases?
8. Where in the world are vast water resources still going un-

used? In what part of the world is water power most effectively used?

WHAT TO DO:
1. Out of simple materials, construct a water wheel. Set it up in operation.
2. Ask the librarian to help you locate information on such topics as these. Report on the most interesting aspects.
   a. The Pelton Water Wheel
   b. The Overshot and Undershot Water Wheel
   c. The Tennessee Valley Authority
   d. Boulder Dam
   e. Grand Coulee Dam
   f. Bonneville Dam
   g. Roosevelt Dam
   h. Victoria Falls
   i. The Paraná River and Its Falls
   j. The Orinoco River and Its Falls
3. If possible, visit a hydroelectric plant or ask the manager of such a plant to speak to your class.
4. Arrange a bulletin board display showing the development of water power and its uses.

REFERENCES:
Community Interests. Samuel Berman. Philadelphia, John C. Winston Company, 1938. Pp. 30–39.

Compton's Pictorial Encyclopedia. Chicago, F. B. Compton & Co., 1936. Vol. 15.

Early Men of Science. William Lewis Nida. Chicago, D. C. Heath & Company, 1926. Pp. 180–190.

Electricity Comes to Us. Rose Wyler. New York, Grosset and Dunlap, Inc., 1937. All.

Elementary Science. Book 4. Ellis C. Persing. New York, D. Appleton-Century Company, 1934. Pp. 169–178.

Moving the Earth. Charles Pierce Burton. New York, Henry Holt & Company, 1936. Pp. 152–188.

Our America. Irving R. Melbo. Indianapolis, Ind., Bobbs-Merrill Company, 1937. Pp. 326–348.
Story of Water Supply. Hope Kerr Holway. New York, Harper & Brothers, 1929. Pp. 66–76.
The World Book Encyclopedia. Chicago, Quarrie Company, 1936. Pp. 7670–7673.

APPENDIX B

Summaries of Nine Rotations for Three Grades for the 27 Films, and Tests for the Statistical Significance of the Differences Between the Means of Performance for Experimental Factors 1, 2, and 3

Table 9 A

Summary of Rotation 1 for Grade 4 for the Three Films:
A. *How Nature Protects Animals;* B. *The Mangbetu;* C. *Pygmies of Africa*
Group A (Bellville)   Group B (Zimmerman)   Group C (Howarth)

A	E.F. 1 IT^1 FT^1 C^1 22 41.84 M = 19.84 SD = 13.35 SEM = 2.72	E.F. 2 IT^1 FT^1 C^2 22 58.52 M = 36.52 SD = 8.17 SEM = 1.60	E.F. 3 IT^1 FT^1 C^3 22 67.08 M = 45.08 SD = 11.26 SEM = 2.34
B	E.F. 2 IT^2 FT^2 C^5 25 44.6 M = 19.6 SD = 13.61 SEM = 3.2	E.F. 3 IT^2 FT^2 C^6 25 69 M = 44.0 SD = 11.06 SEM = 2.41	E.F. 1 IT^2 FT^2 C^4 25 41.84 M = 16.84 SD = 13.66 SEM = 2.73
C	E.F. 3 IT^3 FT^3 C^9 16 70.62 M = 54.62 SD = 14.84 SEM = 2.96	E.F. 1 IT^3 FT^3 C^7 16 57.6 M = 41.6 SD = 14.58 SEM = 2.97	E.F. 2 IT^3 FT^3 C^8 16 58.25 M = 42.25 SD = 12.88 SEM = 2.68

E.F. 3−1 $(C^3+C^6+C^9)-(C^1+C^4+C^7) = (143.7)-(78.28) = \frac{65.42}{3} = 21.81$

E.F. 2−1 $(C^2+C^5+C^8)-(C^1+C^4+C^7) = (98.37)-(78.28) = \frac{20.09}{3} = 6.7$

E.F. 3−2 $(C^3+C^6+C^9)-(C^2+C^5+C^8) = (143.7)-(98.37) = \frac{45.33}{3} = 15.11$

Level of Performance E.F. 1 $(SFT^{EF1} \div 3)-(SIT^{EF1} \div 3) = (47.09)-(21) = 26.09$
Level of Performance E.F. 2 $(SFT^{EF2} \div 3)-(SIT^{EF2} \div 3) = (53.79)-(21) = 32.79$
Level of Performance E.F. 3 $(SFT^{EF3} \div 3)-(SIT^{EF3} \div 3) = (68.90)-(21) = 47.90$

Mean SD of E.F. 1 = $(SDM^{C1} + SDM^{C4} + SDM^{C7}) \div 3 = 13.86$
Mean SD of E.F. 2 = $(SDM^{C2} + SDM^{C5} + SDM^{C8}) \div 3 = 11.55$
Mean SD of E.F. 3 = $(SDM^{C3} + SDM^{C6} + SDM^{C9}) \div 3 = 12.38$

APPENDIX B

Table 9 B
Test for the Statistical Significance of the Differences Between the Means of Performance for Experimental Factors 1, 2, and 3

Grade 4 Rotation 1 Films: A. *How Nature Protects Animals*
B. *The Mangbetu*
C. *Pygmies of Africa*

(1) Significance of Difference between Experimental Factors 3 — 1

$$\frac{(C^3 + C^6 + C^9) - (C^1 + C^4 + C^7)}{\sqrt{(SEM^3)^2 + (SEM^6)^2 + (SEM^9)^2 + (SEM^1)^2 + (SEM^4)^2 + (SEM^7)^2}} =$$

$$\frac{65.42}{\sqrt{43.69}} = \frac{65.42}{6.611} = 9.9 \text{ Standard Units}$$

(2) Significance of Difference between Experimental Factors 2 — 1

$$\frac{(C^2 + C^5 + C^8) - (C^1 + C^4 + C^7)}{\sqrt{(SEM^2)^2 + (SEM^5)^2 + (SEM^8)^2 + (SEM^1)^2 + (SEM^4)^2 + (SEM^7)^2}} =$$

$$\frac{20.09}{\sqrt{43.64}} = \frac{20.09}{6.609} = 3.04 \text{ Standard Units}$$

(3) Significance of Difference between Experimental Factors 3 — 2

$$\frac{(C^3 + C^6 + C^9) - (C^2 + C^5 + C^8)}{\sqrt{(SEM^3)^2 + (SEM^6)^2 + (SEM^9)^2 + (SEM^2)^2 + (SEM^5)^2 + (SEM^8)^2}} =$$

$$\frac{45.33}{\sqrt{40.01}} = \frac{45.33}{6.33} = 7.16 \text{ Standard Units}$$

TABLE 10 A

Summary of Rotation 2 for Grade 4 for the Three Films:
A. *Gray Squirrel;* B. *Birds of Prey;* C. *Children of Switzerland*

Group A (Bellville)   Group B (Zimmerman)   Group C (Howarth)

	Group A (Bellville)	Group B (Zimmerman)	Group C (Howarth)
A	E.F. 1 IT^1 FT^1 C^1 28 63.55 M = 35.55 SD = 15.86 SEM = 3.05	E.F. 2 IT^1 FT^1 C^2 28 68.77 M = 40.77 SD = 9.70 SEM = 2.12	E.F. 3 IT^1 FT^1 C^3 28 82.62 M = 54.62 SD = 7.01 SEM = 1.40
B	E.F. 2 IT^2 FT^2 C^5 30 70.38 M = 40.38 SD = 10.21 SEM = 2.04	E.F. 3 IT^2 FT^2 C^6 30 84 M = 54.0 SD = 7.64 SEM = 1.59	E.F. 1 IT^2 FT^2 C^4 30 56.62 M = 26.62 SD = 10.39 SEM = 1.96
C	E.F. 3 IT^3 FT^3 C^9 24 75.08 M = 51.08 SD = 14.80 SEM = 3.08	E.F. 1 IT^3 FT^3 C^7 24 60.28 M = 36.28 SD = 10.48 SEM = 2.34	E.F. 2 IT^3 FT^3 C^8 24 65.92 M = 41.92 SD = 12.65 SEM = 2.63

E.F. 3−1 $(C^3+C^6+C^9)-(C^1+C^4+C^7) = (159.7)-(98.45) = \dfrac{61.25}{3} = 20.42$

E.F. 2−1 $(C^2+C^5+C^8)-(C^1+C^4+C^7) = (123.07)-(98.45) = \dfrac{24.62}{3} = 8.21$

E.F. 3−2 $(C^3+C^6+C^9)-(C^2+C^5+C^8) = (159.7)-(123.07) = \dfrac{36.63}{3} = 12.21$

Level of Performance E.F. 1 $(SFT^{EF1} \div 3)-(SIT^{EF1} \div 3)=(60.15)-(27.33)=32.82$
Level of Performance E.F. 2 $(SFT^{EF2} \div 3)-(SIT^{EF2} \div 3)=(68.36)-(27.33)=41.03$
Level of Performance E.F. 3 $(SFT^{EF3} \div 3)-(SIT^{EF3} \div 3)=(80.57)-(27.33)=53.24$

    Mean SD of E.F. 1 = $(SDM^{C1} + SDM^{C4} + SDM^{C7}) \div 3 = 12.24$
    Mean SD of E.F. 2 = $(SDM^{C2} + SDM^{C5} + SDM^{C8}) \div 3 = 10.85$
    Mean SD of E.F. 3 = $(SDM^{C3} + SDM^{C6} + SDM^{C9}) \div 3 = 9.81$

APPENDIX B

TABLE 10 B
Test for the Statistical Significance of the Differences Between the Means of Performance for Experimental Factors 1, 2, and 3

Grade 4 Rotation 2 Films:
A. *Gray Squirrel*
B. *Birds of Prey*
C. *Children of Switzerland*

(1) Significance of Difference between Experimental Factors 3 — 1

$$\frac{(C^3 + C^6 + C^9) - (C^1 + C^4 + C^7)}{\sqrt{(SEM^3)^2 + (SEM^6)^2 + (SEM^9)^2 + (SEM^1)^2 + (SEM^4)^2 + (SEM^7)^2}} =$$

$$\frac{61.25}{\sqrt{32.57}} = \frac{61.25}{5.707} = 10.73 \text{ Standard Units}$$

(2) Significance of Difference between Experimental Factors 2 — 1

$$\frac{(C^2 + C^5 + C^8) - (C^1 + C^4 + C^7)}{\sqrt{(SEM^2)^2 + (SEM^5)^2 + (SEM^8)^2 + (SEM^1)^2 + (SEM^4)^2 + (SEM^7)^2}} =$$

$$\frac{24.62}{\sqrt{34.17}} = \frac{24.62}{5.845} = 4.21 \text{ Standard Units}$$

(3) Significance of Difference between Experimental Factors 3 — 2

$$\frac{(C^3 + C^6 + C^9) - (C^2 + C^5 + C^8)}{\sqrt{(SEM^3)^2 + (SEM^6)^2 + (SEM^9)^2 + (SEM^2)^2 + (SEM^5)^2 + (SEM^8)^2}} =$$

$$\frac{36.63}{\sqrt{29.52}} = \frac{36.63}{5.433} = 6.74 \text{ Standard Units}$$

Table II A

Summary of Rotation 3 for Grade 4 for the Three Films:
A. *Moths;* B. *Pond Insects;* C. *The Honey Bee*

Group A (Bellville)   Group B (Zimmerman)   Group C (Howarth)

A	E.F. 1 IT^1 FT^1 C^1 26 50.41 M = 24.41 SD = 11.84 SEM = 2.47	E.F. 2 IT^1 FT^1 C^2 26 66.38 M = 40.38 SD = 8.85 SEM = 1.98	E.F. 3 IT^1 FT^1 C^3 26 79.84 M = 53.84 SD = 9.11 SEM = 1.82
B	E.F. 2 IT^2 FT^2 C^5 23 64.36 M = 41.36 SD = 11.13 SEM = 2.14	E.F. 3 IT^2 FT^2 C^6 23 75.69 M = 52.69 SD = 10.38 SEM = 2.07	E.F. 1 IT^2 FT^2 C^4 23 50.44 M = 27.44 SD = 12.57 SEM = 2.46
C	E.F. 3 IT^3 FT^3 C^9 19 86.56 M = 67.56 SD = 8.25 SEM = 1.69	E.F. 1 IT^3 FT^3 C^7 19 56.44 M = 37.44 SD = 14.88 SEM = 3.03	E.F. 2 IT^3 FT^3 C^8 19 75.11 M = 56.11 SD = 11.24 SEM = 2.20

E.F. 3−1 $(C^3+C^6+C^9)-(C^1+C^4+C^7) = (174.09)-(89.29) = \dfrac{84.8}{3} = 28.27$

E.F. 2−1 $(C^2+C^5+C^8)-(C^1+C^4+C^7) = (137.85)-(89.29) = \dfrac{48.56}{3} = 16.19$

E.F. 3−2 $(C^3+C^6+C^9)-(C^2+C^5+C^8) = (174.09)-(137.85) = \dfrac{36.24}{3} = 12.08$

Level of Performance E.F. 1 $(SFT^{EF1} \div 3)-(SIT^{EF1} \div 3) = (52.43)-(22.66) = 29.77$
Level of Performance E.F. 2 $(SFT^{EF2} \div 3)-(SIT^{EF2} \div 3) = (68.62)-(22.66) = 45.96$
Level of Performance E.F. 3 $(SFT^{EF3} \div 3)-(SIT^{EF3} \div 3) = (80.70)-(22.66) = 58.04$

    Mean SD of E.F. 1 = $(SDM^{C1} + SDM^{C4} + SDM^{C7}) \div 3 = 13.10$
    Mean SD of E.F. 2 = $(SDM^{C2} + SDM^{C5} + SDM^{C8}) \div 3 = 10.41$
    Mean SD of E.F. 3 = $(SDM^{C3} + SDM^{C6} + SDM^{C9}) \div 3 = 9.25$

APPENDIX B

Table 11 B
Test for the Statistical Significance of the Differences Between the Means of Performance for Experimental Factors 1, 2, and 3

Grade 4 Rotation 3 Films: A. *Moths*
B. *Pond Insects*
C. *The Honey Bee*

(1) Significance of Difference between Experimental Factors 3 — 1

$$\frac{(C^3 + C^6 + C^9) - (C^1 + C^4 + C^7)}{\sqrt{(SEM^3)^2 + (SEM^6)^2 + (SEM^9)^2 + (SEM^1)^2 + (SEM^4)^2 + (SEM^7)^2}} =$$

$$\frac{84.8}{\sqrt{31.77}} = \frac{84.8}{5.636} = 15.05 \text{ Standard Units}$$

(2) Significance of Difference between Experimental Factors 2 — 1

$$\frac{(C^2 + C^5 + C^8) - (C^1 + C^4 + C^7)}{\sqrt{(SEM^2)^2 + (SEM^5)^2 + (SEM^8)^2 + (SEM^1)^2 + (SEM^4)^2 + (SEM^7)^2}} =$$

$$\frac{48.56}{\sqrt{34.66}} = \frac{48.56}{5.887} = 8.25 \text{ Standard Units}$$

(3) Significance of Difference between Experimental Factors 3 — 2

$$\frac{(C^3 + C^6 + C^9) - (C^2 + C^5 + C^8)}{\sqrt{(SEM^3)^2 + (SEM^6)^2 + (SEM^9)^2 + (SEM^2)^2 + (SEM^5)^2 + (SEM^8)^2}} =$$

$$\frac{36.24}{\sqrt{23.77}} = \frac{36.24}{4.875} = 7.43 \text{ Standard Units}$$

Table 12 A

Summary of Rotation 1 for Grade 5 for the Three Films:
A. *Airplane Trip;* B. *Old Louisiana;* C. *Transportation*

Group A (Stocker)   Group B (Bolton)   Group C (Heyl)

	Group A (Stocker)	Group B (Bolton)	Group C (Heyl)
A	E.F. 1 IT^1 FT^1 C^1 28 73.04 M = 45.04 SD = 10.34 SEM = 2.11	E.F. 2 IT^1 FT^1 C^2 28 77.36 M = 49.36 SD = 8.88 SEM = 1.71	E.F. 3 IT^1 FT^1 C^3 28 92.41 M = 64.41 SD = 4.67 SEM = 0.97
B	E.F. 2 IT^2 FT^2 C^5 19 56.26 M = 37.26 SD = 13.97 SEM = 2.97	E.F. 3 IT^2 FT^2 C^6 19 67.08 M = 48.08 SD = 14.44 SEM = 3.01	E.F. 1 IT^2 FT^2 C^4 19 48.60 M = 29.60 SD = 12.38 SEM = 2.64
C	E.F. 3 IT^3 FT^3 C^9 30 66.81 M = 36.81 SD = 10.80 SEM = 2.35	E.F. 1 IT^3 FT^3 C^7 30 50.35 M = 20.35 SD = 10.94 SEM = 2.28	E.F. 2 IT^3 FT^3 C^8 30 60.15 M = 30.15 SD = 13.92 SEM = 2.78

E.F. 3−1 $(C^3+C^6+C^9)-(C^1+C^4+C^7) = (149.3)-(94.99) = \frac{54.31}{3} = 18.1$

E.F. 2−1 $(C^2+C^5+C^8)-(C^1+C^4+C^7) = (116.77)-(94.99) = \frac{21.78}{3} = 7.26$

E.F. 3−2 $(C^3+C^6+C^9)-(C^2+C^5+C^8) = (149.30)-(116.77) = \frac{32.53}{3} = 10.84$

Level of Performance E.F. 1 $(SFT^{EF1} \div 3)-(SIT^{EF1} \div 3) = (57.33)-(25.66) = 31.67$
Level of Performance E.F. 2 $(SFT^{EF2} \div 3)-(SIT^{EF2} \div 3) = (64.59)-(25.66) = 38.93$
Level of Performance E.F. 3 $(SFT^{EF3} \div 3)-(SIT^{EF3} \div 3) = (75.43)-(25.66) = 49.77$

Mean SD of E.F. 1 = $(SDM^{C1} + SDM^{C4} + SDM^{C7}) \div 3 = 11.22$
Mean SD of E.F. 2 = $(SDM^{C2} + SDM^{C5} + SDM^{C8}) \div 3 = 12.25$
Mean SD of E.F. 3 = $(SDM^{C3} + SDM^{C6} + SDM^{C9}) \div 3 = 9.97$

APPENDIX B

TABLE 12 B

Test for the Statistical Significance of the Differences Between the Means of Performance for Experimental Factors 1, 2, and 3

Grade 5   Rotation 1   Films: A. *Airplane Trip*
                                             B. *Life in Old Louisiana*
                                             C. *Development of Transportation*

(1) Significance of Difference between Experimental Factors 3 − 1

$$\frac{(C^3 + C^6 + C^9) - (C^1 + C^4 + C^7)}{\sqrt{(SEM^3)^2 + (SEM^6)^2 + (SEM^9)^2 + (SEM^1)^2 + (SEM^4)^2 + (SEM^7)^2}} =$$

$$\frac{54.31}{\sqrt{32.12}} = \frac{54.31}{5.67} = 9.57 \text{ Standard Units}$$

(2) Significance of Difference between Experimental Factors 2 − 1

$$\frac{(C^2 + C^5 + C^8) - (C^1 + C^4 + C^7)}{\sqrt{(SEM^2)^2 + (SEM^5)^2 + (SEM^8)^2 + (SEM^1)^2 + (SEM^4)^2 + (SEM^7)^2}} =$$

$$\frac{21.78}{\sqrt{36.06}} = \frac{21.78}{6.004} = 3.63 \text{ Standard Units}$$

(3) Significance of Difference between Experimental Factors 3 − 2

$$\frac{(C^3 + C^6 + C^9) - (C^2 + C^5 + C^8)}{\sqrt{(SEM^3)^2 + (SEM^6)^2 + (SEM^9)^2 + (SEM^2)^2 + (SEM^5)^2 + (SEM^8)^2}} =$$

$$\frac{32.53}{\sqrt{34.95}} = \frac{32.53}{5.914} = 5.50 \text{ Standard Units}$$

TABLE 13 A

Summary of Rotation 2 for Grade 5 for the Three Films:
A. *Planter of Colonial Virginia;* B. *Arts and Crafts of Mexico;* C. *Pioneers of the Plains*

	Group A (Stocker)	Group B (Bolton)	Group C (Heyl)
A	E.F. 1 IT^1 FT^1 C^1 22 55.52 M = 33.52 SD = 8.56 SEM = 1.75	E.F. 2 IT^1 FT^1 C^2 22 61.77 M = 39.77 SD = 15.56 SEM = 3.11	E.F. 3 IT^1 FT^1 C^3 22 82.48 M = 60.48 SD = 9.83 SEM = 2.01
B	E.F. 2 IT^2 FT^2 C^5 22 58.25 M = 36.25 SD = 14.49 SEM = 3.02	E.F. 3 IT^2 FT^2 C^6 22 73.55 M = 51.55 SD = 13.44 SEM = 2.63	E.F. 1 IT^2 FT^2 C^4 22 49.11 M = 27.11 SD = 14.36 SEM = 2.76
C	E.F. 3 IT^3 FT^3 C^9 22 75.55 M = 53.55 SD = 12.78 SEM = 2.45	E.F. 1 IT^3 FT^3 C^7 22 62.29 M = 40.29 SD = 14.09 SEM = 2.76	E.F. 2 IT^3 FT^3 C^8 22 70.61 M = 48.61 SD = 12.03 SEM = 2.56

E.F. 3−1 $(C^3+C^6+C^9)-(C^1+C^4+C^7) = (165.58)-(100.92) = \frac{64.66}{3} = 21.55$

E.F. 2−1 $(C^2+C^5+C^8)-(C^1+C^4+C^7) = (124.63)-(100.92) = \frac{23.71}{3} = 7.90$

E.F. 3−2 $(C^3+C^6+C^9)-(C^2+C^5+C^8) = (165.58)-(124.63) = \frac{40.95}{3} = 13.65$

Level of Performance E.F. 1 $(SFT^{EF1}\div 3)-(SIT^{EF1}\div 3)=(55.64)-(22)=33.64$
Level of Performance E.F. 2 $(SFT^{EF2}\div 3)-(SIT^{EF2}\div 3)=(63.54)-(22)=41.54$
Level of Performance E.F. 3 $(SFT^{EF3}\div 3)-(SIT^{EF3}\div 3)=(77.19)-(22)=55.19$

Mean SD of E.F. 1 = $(SDM^{C1} + SDM^{C4} + SDM^{C7}) \div 3 = 12.33$
Mean SD of E.F. 2 = $(SDM^{C2} + SDM^{C5} + SDM^{C8}) \div 3 = 14.02$
Mean SD of E.F. 3 = $(SDM^{C3} + SDM^{C6} + SDM^{C9}) \div 3 = 12.01$

APPENDIX B

TABLE 13 B
Test for the Statistical Significance of the Differences Between the Means of Performance for Experimental Factors 1, 2, and 3

Grade 5   Rotation 2   Films: A. *Planter of Colonial Virginia*
B. *Arts and Crafts of Mexico*
C. *Pioneers of the Plains*

(1) Significance of Difference between Experimental Factors 3 — 1

$$\frac{(C^3 + C^6 + C^9) - (C^1 + C^4 + C^7)}{\sqrt{(SEM^3)^2 + (SEM^6)^2 + (SEM^9)^2 + (SEM^1)^2 + (SEM^4)^2 + (SEM^7)^2}} =$$

$$\frac{64.66}{\sqrt{35.23}} = \frac{64.66}{5.933} = 10.89 \text{ Standard Units}$$

(2) Significance of Difference between Experimental Factors 2 — 1

$$\frac{(C^2 + C^5 + C^8) - (C^1 + C^4 + C^7)}{\sqrt{(SEM^2)^2 + (SEM^5)^2 + (SEM^8)^2 + (SEM^1)^2 + (SEM^4)^2 + (SEM^7)^2}} =$$

$$\frac{23.71}{\sqrt{43.62}} = \frac{23.71}{6.604} = 3.6 \text{ Standard Units}$$

(3) Significance of Difference between Experimental Factors 3 — 2

$$\frac{(C^3 + C^6 + C^9) - (C^2 + C^5 + C^8)}{\sqrt{(SEM^3)^2 + (SEM^6)^2 + (SEM^9)^2 + (SEM^2)^2 + (SEM^5)^2 + (SEM^8)^2}} =$$

$$\frac{40.95}{\sqrt{42.29}} = \frac{40.95}{6.503} = 6.3 \text{ Standard Units}$$

Table 14 A

Summary of Rotation 3 for Grade 5 for the Three Films:
A. *Land of Mexico;* B. *The Truck Farmer;* C. *Irrigation Farming*

	Group A (Stocker)	Group B (Bolton)	Group C (Heyl)
A	E.F. 1 IT^1 FT^1 C^1 18 49.48 M = 31.38 SD = 10.63 SEM = 2.08	E.F. 2 IT^1 FT^1 C^2 18 67.48 M = 49.48 SD = 11.56 SEM = 2.26	E.F. 3 IT^1 FT^1 C^3 18 83.6 M = 65.6 SD = 9.15 SEM = 1.86
B	E.F. 2 IT^2 FT^2 C^5 25 78.08 M = 53.08 SD = 7.79 SEM = 1.66	E.F. 3 IT^2 FT^2 C^6 25 85.09 M = 60.09 SD = 7.55 SEM = 1.64	E.F. 1 IT^2 FT^2 C^4 25 65.25 M = 40.25 SD = 11.13 SEM = 2.32
C	E.F. 3 IT^3 FT^3 C^9 22 73.65 M = 51.65 SD = 8.8 SEM = 1.87	E.F. 1 IT^3 FT^3 C^7 22 39.76 M = 17.76 SD = 9.45 SEM = 1.89	E.F. 2 IT^3 FT^3 C^8 22 60.72 M = 38.72 SD = 9.34 SEM = 1.91

E.F. 3−1 $(C^3+C^6+C^9)-(C^1+C^4+C^7) = (177.34)-(89.39) = \frac{87.95}{3} = 29.32$

E.F. 2−1 $(C^2+C^5+C^8)-(C^1+C^4+C^7) = (141.28)-(89.39) = \frac{51.89}{3} = 17.30$

E.F. 3−2 $(C^3+C^6+C^9)-(C^2+C^5+C^8) = (177.34)-(141.28) = \frac{36.06}{3} = 12.02$

Level of Performance E.F. 1 $(SFT^{EF1}\div3)-(SIT^{EF1}\div3)=(51.50)-(21.67)=29.83$
Level of Performance E.F. 2 $(SFT^{EF2}\div3)-(SIT^{EF2}\div3)=(68.76)-(21.67)=47.09$
Level of Performance E.F. 3 $(SFT^{EF3}\div3)-(SIT^{EF3}\div3)=(80.78)-(21.67)=59.11$

Mean SD of E.F. 1 = $(SDM^{C1} + SDM^{C4} + SDM^{C7}) \div 3 = 10.40$
Mean SD of E.F. 2 = $(SDM^{C2} + SDM^{C5} + SDM^{C8}) \div 3 = 9.56$
Mean SD of E.F. 3 = $(SDM^{C3} + SDM^{C6} + SDM^{C9}) \div 3 = 8.5$

Appendix B

Table 14 B
Test for the Statistical Significance of the Differences Between the Means of Performance for Experimental Factors 1, 2, and 3

Grade 5 Rotation 3 Films: A. *Land of Mexico*
B. *The Truck Farmer*
C. *Irrigation Farming*

(1) Significance of Difference between Experimental Factors 3 — 1

$$\frac{(C^3 + C^6 + C^9) - (C^1 + C^4 + C^7)}{\sqrt{(SEM^3)^2 + (SEM^6)^2 + (SEM^9)^2 + (SEM^1)^2 + (SEM^4)^2 + (SEM^7)^2}} =$$

$$\frac{87.95}{\sqrt{22.89}} = \frac{87.95}{4.784} = 18.38 \text{ Standard Units}$$

(2) Significance of Difference between Experimental Factors 2 — 1

$$\frac{(C^2 + C^5 + C^8) - (C^1 + C^4 + C^7)}{\sqrt{(SEM^2)^2 + (SEM^5)^2 + (SEM^8)^2 + (SEM^1)^2 + (SEM^4)^2 + (SEM^7)^2}} =$$

$$\frac{51.89}{\sqrt{24.76}} = \frac{51.89}{4.976} = 10.43 \text{ Standard Units}$$

(3) Significance of Difference between Experimental Factors 3 — 2

$$\frac{(C^3 + C^6 + C^9) - (C^2 + C^5 + C^8)}{\sqrt{(SEM^3)^2 + (SEM^6)^2 + (SEM^9)^2 + (SEM^2)^2 + (SEM^5)^2 + (SEM^8)^2}} =$$

$$\frac{36.06}{\sqrt{21.11}} = \frac{36.06}{4.594} = 7.85 \text{ Standard Units}$$

Table 15 A

Summary of Rotation 1 for Grade 6 for the Three Films:
A. *Children of China*; B. *Children of Japan*; C. *People of Hawaii*

	Group A (Ferber)	Group B (Simon)	Group C (Walker)
A	E.F. 1 IT^1 FT^1 C^1 24 62.45 M = 38.45 SD = 10.71 SEM = 2.33	E.F. 2 IT^1 FT^1 C^2 24 74.2 M = 50.2 SD = 8.37 SEM = 1.87	E.F. 3 IT^1 FT^1 C^3 24 89.7 M = 65.7 SD = 4.71 SEM = 1.05
B	E.F. 2 IT^2 FT^2 C^5 21 79.08 M = 58.08 SD = 6.53 SEM = 1.36	E.F. 3 IT^2 FT^2 C^6 21 88.43 M = 67.43 SD = 6.97 SEM = 1.48	E.F. 1 IT^2 FT^2 C^4 21 67.42 M = 46.42 SD = 7.42 SEM = 1.42
C	E.F. 3 IT^3 FT^3 C^9 19 84.95 M = 65.95 SD = 8.02 SEM = 1.71	E.F. 1 IT^3 FT^3 C^7 19 58.26 M = 39.26 SD = 9.26 SEM = 1.97	E.F. 2 IT^3 FT^3 C^8 19 76.84 M = 57.84 SD = 7.51 SEM = 1.5

E.F. 3−1 $(C^3+C^6+C^9)-(C^1+C^4+C^7) = (199.08)-(124.13) = \frac{74.95}{3} = 24.98$

E.F. 2−1 $(C^2+C^5+C^8)-(C^1+C^4+C^7) = (166.12)-(124.13) = \frac{41.99}{3} = 13.99$

E.F. 3−2 $(C^3+C^6+C^9)-(C^2+C^5+C^8) = (199.08)-(166.12) = \frac{32.96}{3} = 10.99$

Level of Performance E.F. 1 $(SFT^{EF1} \div 3)-(SIT^{EF1} \div 3) = (62.7)-(21.33) = 41.37$
Level of Performance E.F. 2 $(SFT^{EF2} \div 3)-(SIT^{EF2} \div 3) = (76.7)-(21.33) = 55.37$
Level of Performance E.F. 3 $(SFT^{EF3} \div 3)-(SIT^{EF3} \div 3) = (87.7)-(21.33) = 66.37$

Mean SD of E.F. 1 = $(SDM^{C1} + SDM^{C4} + SDM^{C7}) \div 3 = 9.13$
Mean SD of E.F. 2 = $(SDM^{C2} + SDM^{C5} + SDM^{C8}) \div 3 = 7.47$
Mean SD of E.F. 3 = $(SDM^{C3} + SDM^{C6} + SDM^{C9}) \div 3 = 6.57$

APPENDIX B

Table 15 B
Test for the Statistical Significance of the Differences Between the Means of Performance for Experimental Factors 1, 2, and 3

Grade 6   Rotation 1   Films: A. *Children of China*
B. *Children of Japan*
C. *People of Hawaii*

(1) Significance of Difference between Experimental Factors 3 — 1

$$\frac{(C^3 + C^6 + C^9) - (C^1 + C^4 + C^7)}{\sqrt{(SEM^3)^2 + (SEM^6)^2 + (SEM^9)^2 + (SEM^1)^2 + (SEM^4)^2 + (SEM^7)^2}} =$$

$$\frac{74.93}{\sqrt{17.5432}} = \frac{74.93}{4.18} = 17.92 \text{ Standard Units}$$

(2) Significance of Difference between Experimental Factors 2 — 1

$$\frac{(C^2 + C^5 + C^8) - (C^1 + C^4 + C^7)}{\sqrt{(SEM^2)^2 + (SEM^5)^2 + (SEM^8)^2 + (SEM^1)^2 + (SEM^4)^2 + (SEM^7)^2}} =$$

$$\frac{41.99}{\sqrt{18.93}} = \frac{41.99}{4.35} = 9.65 \text{ Standard Units}$$

(3) Significance of Difference between Experimental Factors 3 — 2

$$\frac{(C^3 + C^6 + C^9) - (C^2 + C^5 + C^8)}{\sqrt{(SEM^3)^2 + (SEM^6)^2 + (SEM^9)^2 + (SEM^2)^2 + (SEM^5)^2 + (SEM^8)^2}} =$$

$$\frac{32.94}{\sqrt{13.81}} = \frac{32.94}{3.7161} = 8.86 \text{ Standard Units}$$

TABLE 16 A

Summary of Rotation 2 for Grade 6 for the Three Films:
A. *People of Mexico*; B. *Argentina*; C. *Chile*

	Group A (Walker)	Group B (Ferber)	Group C (Simon)
A	E.F. 1 IT^1 FT^1 C^1 17 57.52 M = 40.52 SD = 10.25 SEM = 2.09	E.F. 2 IT^1 FT^1 C^2 17 74.95 M = 57.95 SD = 9.81 SEM = 2.09	E.F. 3 IT^1 FT^1 C^3 17 83.33 M = 66.33 SD = 8.52 SEM = 1.67
B	E.F. 2 IT^2 FT^2 C^5 19 72.23 M = 53.23 SD = 9.14 SEM = 1.83	E.F. 3 IT^2 FT^2 C^6 19 87.4 M = 68.4 SD = 7.26 SEM = 1.42	E.F. 1 IT^2 FT^2 C^4 19 54.07 M = 35.07 SD = 11.83 SEM = 2.36
C	E.F. 3 IT^3 FT^3 C^9 22 80.25 M = 58.25 SD = 7.83 SEM = 1.63	E.F. 1 IT^3 FT^3 C^7 22 51.15 M = 29.15 SD = 7.24 SEM = 1.44	E.F. 2 IT^3 FT^3 C^8 22 68 M = 46.0 SD = 10.4 SEM = 2.04

E.F. 3−1 $(C^3+C^6+C^9)-(C^1+C^4+C^7) = (192.98)-(104.74) = \frac{88.24}{3} = 29.41$

E.F. 2−1 $(C^2+C^5+C^8)-(C^1+C^4+C^7) = (157.18)-(104.74) = \frac{52.44}{3} = 17.48$

E.F. 3−2 $(C^3+C^6+C^9)-(C^2+C^5+C^8) = (192.98)-(157.18) = \frac{35.8}{3} = 11.93$

Level of Performance E.F. 1 $(SFT^{EF1} \div 3)-(SIT^{EF1} \div 3) = (54.24)-(19.33) = 34.91$
Level of Performance E.F. 2 $(SFT^{EF2} \div 3)-(SIT^{EF2} \div 3) = (71.72)-(19.33) = 52.39$
Level of Performance E.F. 3 $(SFT^{EF3} \div 3)-(SIT^{EF3} \div 3) = (83.66)-(19.33) = 64.33$

    Mean SD of E.F. 1 = $(SDM^{C1} + SDM^{C4} + SDM^{C7}) \div 3 = 9.77$
    Mean SD of E.F. 2 = $(SDM^{C2} + SDM^{C5} + SDM^{C8}) \div 3 = 9.78$
    Mean SD of E.F. 3 = $(SDM^{C3} + SDM^{C6} + SDM^{C9}) \div 3 = 7.87$

APPENDIX B

TABLE 16 B

Test for the Statistical Significance of the Differences Between the Means of Performance for Experimental Factors 1, 2, and 3

Grade 6   Rotation 2   Films: A. *People of Mexico*
B. *Argentina*
C. *Chile*

(1) Significance of Difference between Experimental Factors 3 − 1

$$\frac{(C^3 + C^6 + C^9) - (C^1 + C^4 + C^7)}{\sqrt{(SEM^3)^2 + (SEM^6)^2 + (SEM^9)^2 + (SEM^1)^2 + (SEM^4)^2 + (SEM^7)^2}} =$$

$$\frac{88.24}{\sqrt{19.43}} = \frac{88.24}{4.408} = 20.02 \text{ Standard Units}$$

(2) Significance of Difference between Experimental Factors 2 − 1

$$\frac{(C^2 + C^5 + C^8) - (C^1 + C^4 + C^7)}{\sqrt{(SEM^2)^2 + (SEM^5)^2 + (SEM^8)^2 + (SEM^1)^2 + (SEM^4)^2 + (SEM^7)^2}} =$$

$$\frac{52.44}{\sqrt{23.85}} = \frac{52.44}{4.884} = 10.73 \text{ Standard Units}$$

(3) Significance of Difference between Experimental Factors 3 − 2

$$\frac{(C^3 + C^6 + C^9) - (C^2 + C^5 + C^8)}{\sqrt{(SEM^3)^2 + (SEM^6)^2 + (SEM^9)^2 + (SEM^2)^2 + (SEM^5)^2 + (SEM^8)^2}} =$$

$$\frac{35.8}{\sqrt{19.30}} = \frac{35.8}{4.39} = 8.15 \text{ Standard Units}$$

Table 17 A
Summary of Rotation 3 for Grade 6 for the Three Films:
A. *Peru*; B. *Water Power*; C. *Simple Machines*

	Group A (Simon)	Group B (Walker)	Group C (Ferber)
A	E.F. 1 IT^1 FT^1 C^1 24 57.53 M = 33.53 SD = 12.51 SEM = 2.50	E.F. 2 IT^1 FT^1 C^2 24 75.04 M = 51.04 SD = 7.25 SEM = 1.48	E.F. 3 IT^1 FT^1 C^3 24 85.03 M = 61.03 SD = 7.45 SEM = 1.46
B	E.F. 2 IT^2 FT^2 C^5 16 59.11 M = 43.11 SD = 10.03 SEM = 1.97	E.F. 3 IT^2 FT^2 C^6 16 68.46 M = 52.46 SD = 13.47 SEM = 2.69	E.F. 1 IT^2 FT^2 C^4 16 43.23 M = 27.23 SD = 12.58 SEM = 2.52
C	E.F. 3 IT^3 FT^3 C^9 14 67.51 M = 53.51 SD = 10.21 SEM = 1.93	E.F. 1 IT^3 FT^3 C^7 14 37.0 M = 23.0 SD = 13.46 SEM = 2.69	E.F. 2 IT^3 FT^3 C^8 14 54.51 M = 40.51 SD = 10.73 SEM = 2.11

E.F. 3−1 $(C^3+C^6+C^9)-(C^1+C^4+C^7) = (167)-(83.76) = \frac{83.24}{3} = 27.74$

E.F. 2−1 $(C^2+C^5+C^8)-(C^1+C^4+C^7) = (134.66)-(83.76) = \frac{50.90}{3} = 16.96$

E.F. 3−2 $(C^3+C^6+C^9)-(C^2+C^5+C^8) = (167)-(134.66) = \frac{32.34}{3} = 10.78$

Level of Performance E.F. 1 $(SFT^{EF1} \div 3)-(SIT^{EF1} \div 3) = (45.92)-(18) = 27.92$
Level of Performance E.F. 2 $(SFT^{EF2} \div 3)-(SIT^{EF2} \div 3) = (62.89)-(18) = 44.89$
Level of Performance E.F. 3 $(SFT^{EF3} \div 3)-(SIT^{EF3} \div 3) = (73.67)-(18) = 55.67$

Mean SD of E.F. 1 = $(SDM^{C1} + SDM^{C4} + SDM^{C7}) \div 3 = 12.85$
Mean SD of E.F. 2 = $(SDM^{C2} + SDM^{C5} + SDM^{C8}) \div 3 = 9.34$
Mean SD of E.F. 3 = $(SDM^{C3} + SDM^{C6} + SDM^{C9}) \div 3 = 10.38$

APPENDIX B

TABLE 17 B
Test for the Statistical Significance of the Differences Between the Means of Performance for Experimental Factors 1, 2, and 3

Grade 6   Rotation 3   Films: A. *Peru*
B. *Water Power*
C. *Simple Machines*

(1) Significance of Difference between Experimental Factors 3 − 1

$$\frac{(C^3 + C^6 + C^9) - (C^1 + C^4 + C^7)}{\sqrt{(SEM^3)^2 + (SEM^6)^2 + (SEM^9)^2 + (SEM^1)^2 + (SEM^4)^2 + (SEM^7)^2}} =$$

$$\frac{83.24}{\sqrt{32.91}} = \frac{83.24}{5.73} = 14.52 \text{ Standard Units}$$

(2) Significance of Difference between Experimental Factors 2 − 1

$$\frac{(C^2 + C^5 + C^8) - (C^1 + C^4 + C^7)}{\sqrt{(SEM^2)^2 + (SEM^5)^2 + (SEM^8)^2 + (SEM^1)^2 + (SEM^4)^2 + (SEM^7)^2}} =$$

$$\frac{50.90}{\sqrt{30.35}} = \frac{50.90}{5.5} = 9.25 \text{ Standard Units}$$

(3) Significance of Difference between Experimental Factors 3 − 2

$$\frac{(C^3 + C^6 + C^9) - (C^2 + C^5 + C^8)}{\sqrt{(SEM^3)^2 + (SEM^6)^2 + (SEM^9)^2 + (SEM^2)^2 + (SEM^5)^2 + (SEM^8)^2}} =$$

$$\frac{32.34}{\sqrt{23.60}} = \frac{32.34}{4.86} = 6.65 \text{ Standard Units}$$

www.ingramcontent.com/pod-product-compliance
Lightning Source LLC
Chambersburg PA
CBHW051102230426
43667CB00013B/2410